DATSUN Z
240Z/260Z/280Z

James Morris

CONTENTS

Foulis

Haynes

ISBN 0 85429 488 0

A FOULIS Motoring Book

First published 1986

© **Haynes Publishing Group**

Published by:
Haynes Publishing Group,
Sparkford, Nr. Yeovil,
Somerset BS22 7JJ

Haynes Publications Inc.
861 Lawrence Drive, Newbury
Park, California 91320 USA

Library of Congress Catalog Card Number

85-82154

Editor: Mansur Darlington
Cover design: Rowland Smith
Page layout: Chris Hull
Photographs: Andrew Morland,
and author
Road tests: Courtesy of *Motor,*
Autocar and *Autosport*
Printed in England by:
J.H. Haynes & Co. Ltd

Titles in the *Super Profile* series

Further titles in this series will be published at regular
intervals. For information on new titles please contact
your bookseller or write to the publisher.

FOREWORD

The Datsun Z series of sportscars holds a most important place in motoring history. The international mass production sportscar market had, for many years, been virtually completely in European hands. Marques like MG, Austin-Healey, Triumph had, along with Opel and Fiat, dominated the market place, particularly the lucrative American market. The establishment was in for a shock. The Japanese had their eye on this market and, in the same way that they took over the hi-fi, television, video and motor cycle industries, they moved into sportscars. As with the other industries they did the job properly and produced a car with styling, performance, handling and equipment so superior that it simply outsold every other sportscar ever made. After years in the doldrums with staid and outdated sportscars, the owners were becoming tired of being left behind by family saloons both at the traffic lights and on twisty roads, so the Z's success was not really surprising.

The market place was thrown open again as the world's car makers, stunned by the success of the Z, took up the challenge to win a slice of the cake for themselves. MG and Triumph, due undoubtedly to lack of investment from the ailing BL, could come up with nothing with which to compete and were eventually forced to close, their markets lost. A classic example of the survival of the fittest. Other manufacturers, notably those from Japan, fared much better, as did Porsche who answered the Z's challenge with the 924.

There was never anything revolutionary about the Z's basic design; a front-engined, rear wheel drive, two-seater coupé. It had been done many times before, but nobody had ever got it right before. Datsun launched it into the market having no real sportscar pedigree, history or competition successes with which to provide the right image. Datsun knew enough about marketing to realize that this was a vital point, so they set about building an image by entering into motorsport. They embarked directly with a programme of international rallying with a full works team, and indirectly via Peter Brock's BRE racing team in the States. Successes followed, and the resulting publicity quickly presented an enviable competition record to back up the car's sporting image which inevitably led directly to increased sales. The figures show a growth from around 13,000 cars in 1970 to 80,000 in 1977 – the last full year in which the Z was sold – and a grand total of 542,208 cars!

In writing this book I have had a good deal of fun, particularly in the research where I met,

corresponded with and talked to many interesting people, and I should like to thank them for taking the trouble to assist my efforts. My thanks particularly to members of the Z Club who took time to answer my questions, and to send me photos, press cuttings, even a full spare parts catalogue, and who arrived *en masse* from every part of the country in response to my call for the best examples to attend a photo session. My gratitude also to Hamish Cardno of Nissan UK for obtaining some excellent photos from Nissan's archives in Japan with which to illustrate the Z in competition; to *Motor, Autocar* and *Autosport* for permission to reproduce their articles; to Andrew Morland for photographing the Z Club's cars; and to Spike Anderson for telling me the Samuri story. Last, but by no means least, my thanks to my long-suffering wife, Patricia, for preparing the manuscript and for putting up with my preoccupation as well as a constantly ringing telephone.

James Morris

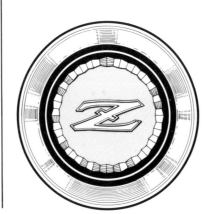

HISTORY

Had you, in the early nineteen-seventies, asked almost anyone to name successful mass market sportscar manufacturers, one name which was unlikely to be mentioned was Datsun. Yet the Nissan Motor Company of Yokohama has been producing sportscars since the late nineteen-fifties. The first Datsun sportscars can, due to their very short production lives and rapid specification changes, be seen virtually as experiments. The first model, the SP211, came onto the Japanese market in 1959. An open 2 + 2 with fibre-glass body – unusual for the time – and the 34bhp 998cc engine and running gear from the 210 saloon. The SP211 soon gave way to the SPL212, differing from the earlier model in using the Bluebird's 1189cc, 48bhp engine. This model was followed very rapidly by the SPL213, basically the same car, but with the power output raised to 55bhp. These three models had a total life span of some 3¹/2 years, with total sales of only 500 examples; but Datsun were learning, and learning fast. Their knowledge was being put to good use as a new and much more sophisticated model was under development, the Fairlady SP310. The new model was launched

at the Tokyo Motor Show in 1961, and went on sale the following year, within a few months of the all-new MGB. The British offering was superior and was responsible for the Datsun's sales being limited to around 7000 vehicles.

A most unusual feature of the SP310 was the fact that it was a three-seater, the rear passenger being seated behind and at 90 degrees to the front seats on the right-hand side. There was virtually no footwell, and this unsuccessful feature was discontinued in 1963 at which time the power output was lifted by 9bhp to 80bhp.

The Fairlady was subject to constant development and, during 1965, the SP310 was superseded by the SP311. Outwardly the same as its predecessor, and known as the Fairlady 1600, the new model boasted a 1595cc, 90bhp engine, front disc brakes and an all-synchromesh gearbox which improved the car's performance and put it clearly in the MGB class.

Development continued and, in 1967, a new model using the same chassis and body as the SP311 was introduced to sell alongside it. The SR311 or Fairlady 2000 was a cut above the MG in both performance and specification, having a 1982cc single overhead cam engine giving some 145bhp and a five-speed all synchromesh gearbox. Top speed was claimed as 125mph with a 0 – 60mph time of around 9 seconds. Datsun never sold this, or any other Fairlady model, in England but a few SR311s were sold in Europe following interest shown as a result of the entries made in the 1968 and 1969 Monte Carlo Rallies.

The Fairlady models were quite successful, particularly in America where most of the 47,000 vehicles produced were sold. This success should have set alarm bells ringing and warning lights flashing for the world's sportscar manufacturers but, for some reason, they failed to take the

Japanese challenge seriously. They were forced to sit up and take notice, however, when, in November 1969 at the Tokyo Motor Show, Datsun unveiled their new weapon, the Fairlady Z.

To develop the new car, Nissan had secured the services of the German industrial Designer, Count Albrecht Goertz, who having lived largely in America since the nineteen-thirties, had a thorough understanding of the requirements of the US market. Goertz had previously designed two cars for BMW; the 503 cabriolet and the 507 sports coupé of 1955. He had also worked for Porsche on the development of the 911, so his credentials were good. His first project for Nissan was the Silvia, a 2 + 2 coupé which was launched in 1964. It was not successful, production ceasing after only 550 had been made. By this time, the initial stages of the Z's design were well under way.

The concept which Goertz had settled on was for a stylish two-seater fixed-head coupé with a lot of Corvette, Porsche and Ferrari influences. The front-end treatment of the Goertz prototype was rather similar to the early sixties Corvette Stingray, having very similar pop-up headlights and a pronounced point to the bonnet. The sharply cut-off rear was pure Italian, and yet rather similar to the way the DBS Aston Martin turned out, while the roof line and overall dimensions seem Porsche 911 influenced. Interestingly, Goertz settled for a traditional boot built into the sloping rear, and wire wheels with knock-on hubs – very sixties.

Nissan had contracted the prototype building to Yamaha who had designed and built a 2-litre twin cam engine especially for the car. A full prototype was built but, when it became clear that there were numerous technical problems, Nissan pulled out and the whole project was shelved.

Some two years later, in 1966, and after Nissan and Goertz had parted company, the project was brought out of mothballs and the Nissan design team set to work to rehash the design. A number of styles were developed to full size clay models but, try as they might, the outcome was never as good as the abandoned Yamaha prototype of which Goertz had headed the development.

The Nissan design team returned to the Goertz concept car and redeveloped it, both from a styling and mechanical point of view. The front end was changed to eliminate the pop-up headlights, the result being an exaggerated version of the E Type's 'sugar scoops'. The pointed nose was blunted somewhat, the bonnet extended fully to the front edge instead of fitting into a cut-out, the boot became a hatch back, and steel wheels with rather nasty hub caps replaced the spoked wheels. Many other detail changes were made, but the essential character of Goertz' design was retained.

In common with sportscars from the world's major motor manufacturers, Nissan took or adapted many of its mechanical components from existing production vehicles. The single overhead camshaft engine was a six-cylinder version of the 1595cc unit employed in the 510 Bluebird saloon; more precisely it was derived from the high performance 510 SSS which had larger valves, a higher compression ratio and a different cam profile to the basic 510. The Bluebird engine was in turn a four-cylinder version of the Mercedes six-cylinder unit, the design of which was licensed to Prince Motors whom Nissan had bought out a few years earlier. Look under the bonnet of an early sixties Mercedes 220 and it's like looking at a Z engine. The quality of the unit is clear.

The Z's L24 engine is a very straightforward in-line six-cylinder unit; the block is cast iron and the aluminium cylinder head gives a 9.0:1 compression. The forged crank runs in seven main bearings

of exceptionally large diameter, and the single overhead camshaft is driven by a Duplex chain from the front of the crank. A second gear, also at the front of the crankshaft, meshes onto a diagonal shaft which drives the oil pump at the bottom and the distributor at the top. Fuel is supplied via a mechanical pump driven off the front of the cam to two Hitachi-SU HJG46W (46mm) carburettors.

Power output from this exceptionally smooth engine was given as 150bhp and, due to its oversquare bore and stroke relationship, it is a very willing revver. Nissan felt safe, therefore, to red line the unit at 7000rpm, the amber starting at 6500. Being a high revving unit has not had any detrimental effect on its longevity, history having proved it to be extremely long lived, and engine failures are rare indeed. Nissan equipped the engine with a viscous coupling for the fan drive. This served two purposes; firstly in reducing power loss, and secondly in lessening fan noise at high revs.

The five-speed gearbox, standard in most markets but an option in the US, was taken directly from the SR311 Fairlady 2000. The American four-speed 'box was simply a revised 510 Bluebird unit, but with strengthened internals to cope with the Z's extra power, and revised ratios to make the most of the engine's power band. Both gearboxes were all-synchromesh and drove through a conventional single dry-plate clutch, via a universally-jointed prop shaft, to a chassis-mounted differential.

Suspension was fully independent at both front and rear. At the front the MacPherson struts are located at the top by turrets, and at the bottom by pivoted track control arms onto the transverse crossmember which, in turn, bolts through rubber insulators to the main front structural rails. Fore and aft location is aided by lower rearward-facing radius rods. The major components are common to

the 1800 saloon, which was in turn derived from the 510 Bluebird. Steering is by rack and pinion of 2.7 turns lock-to-lock, which is unique to the Z. An anti-roll bar is also fitted, varying in thickness according to market.

Rear suspension, also by strut, is unique to the Z, located on large lower A-arms which in turn pivot on the differential mounting's subframe. Drive is provided by double constant velocity jointed shafts. An anti-roll bar is fitted for some markets.

Braking is dual circuit, 10.7 inch disc front and 9 x 1 $\frac{5}{8}$ inch rear finned aluminium drums. The rear brakes were taken directly from the Fairlady 2000 and a vacuum servo unit fitted.

Many other small items such as door handles, locks and wing-mounted indicators were taken from stock.

For so long, sportscars in general had been draughty, uncomfortable, cramped and generally lacking in creature comforts. Both Goertz and Nissan understood the need for the new model to provide something better for an increasingly sophisticated buying public. Goertz replaced the rather diminutive Japanese dummies, around which interiors are designed, with much taller ones so as to arrive at an interior which would be sufficiently spacious for the generally larger built customers at whom Nissan were aiming the vehicle. This enabled a driver of any size, with the aid of the reclining high backed seats, to achieve a driving position second to none.

To assist in their efforts to provide a new car which had all the right equipment, Nissan commissioned extensive market research in America. They used the information obtained to provide the prospective purchaser with a long list of features which their studies had indicated were considered important. These consisted of a sculptured and fully instrumented dash with ammeter, oil pressure, fuel and water temperature gauges alongside an 8000rpm tachometer, 160mph speedometer and a clock. Instrument lighting was adjustable for brightness via a rheostat knob, and the speedometer featured an odometer. Creature comforts included two separate ventilation systems. The first offered normal heating/ventilation, either to the feet or the screen, and cool air only via a central fascia outlet, plus the usual eyeball vent at each end. The second system, operated by pull knobs under each end of the dash, blasted cool air, collected from ahead of the radiator, into either or both footwells by ram effect. Additional items of interest included a signal-seeking radio with electric aerial (optional in some markets), interior/courtesy lights, reclining bucket seats, dipping mirror, an illuminated and lockable glovebox, ashtray, manual choke, hand throttle, map light, two-speed wipers, a wooden gear knob and an imitation wood-rim steering wheel (imitation because in many markets genuine wood rims are illegal due to their behaviour in an accident). The rear luggage area was provided with nylon straps with which to secure suitcases, and there was also a pair of underfloor bins immediately behind the seats for the tool kit and oddments. The driver was given a rest for his clutch foot, and the underbonnet was thoughtfully provided with a lamp fitted with a long 'wander lead'.

So it was with this comprehensively equipped interior, impressive mechanical specification and attractive body that Nissan proudly launched the new model.

The first cars for the all-important American market arrived shortly after the Tokyo Motor Show launch, having been announced there a couple of weeks earlier on 22 October 1969. The press and public were unanimous in their enthusiastic reaction to the all-new model;

many were simply bewildered by the remarkable value for money it offered. This was perhaps best summed up by the opening paragraphs of an article in *Popular Imported Car* magazine, which said:

'Dare we say it? Why not? The Datsun 240-Z is the best all-round sports-GT car we have ever driven that costs less than $6,000. Yes, we know that takes in a lot of territory. Yes, we know that includes most Corvettes, a lot of Porsches including the new 914, the Opel GT, a lot of British machinery and all kinds of other sports-GT cars. But that's the way we feel about it.

'The 240-Z has got to be one of the most happening cars in the past ten years, maybe longer. It's got it all – handling, go-power, looks, comfort and convenience. And with all standard equipment – and that includes an AM signal-seeking radio and power antenna – the list price is only $3526. Don't ask us how they can sell the car for $3526. We don't know. All we know is that they do and you're the benefactor [*sic*].'

In July 1970 *Road & Track* magazine undertook a '$3500 GT' road test where they compared the 240Z with the Opel GT, MGB GT, Triumph GT6 and Fiat 124 Sports. Their test involved five drivers, each driving all the models, and allocating points out of ten to various aspects of the car. When the scores were averaged out it

was found that the 240Z was a clear winner. One road tester commented that the Z should be considered separately as it was simply in a class above the rest. Their test also indicated that the Z came out top on 0 – 60 mph time, top speed, speed at and time over the quarter mile, cornering ability, control in a panic stop and interior space and equipment.

The other major challenger in the international market was the Triumph TR6. The Australian magazine *Sports Cars* published a 'back-to-back' test between the two cars and came out strongly in favour of the Datsun. The TR engine was much admired, as was the coachwork, but they considered the chassis of the Triumph to be very poor, commenting that the TR was 'easily the worst handling sports or performance car we have ever driven....' and summed up that, 'The Z is basically an infinitely better motor car....'

Following press reactions like these, it is hardly surprising that sales took off and Nissan found themselves in the embarrassing, yet enviable, position of being unable to meet the demand. Production had to be geared up from 2000 per month in total to 4000 per month for the US alone, but even so it took almost three years for the waiting lists at dealers to diminish to reasonable levels. The laws of supply and demand took over and dealers took full advantage of the situation to push prices above Nissan's official price. They achieved this by ordering vehicles with many extras and even adding their own, such as alloy wheels, all of which helped to push up prices and profits.

Due to the limited availability, sales for the first year were held down to around 23,000 vehicles, with America taking the lion's share. Sales in following years leaped as more vehicles were made available; 1971 saw 44,000 and in 1972 they exceeded 62,000 worldwide.

The 240Z was first shown to the British public at the 1970 Earls Court Motor Show, and a strong reaction at the Show and to the team of works cars on the RAC Rally a few weeks later, persuaded a disinterested Datsun UK to import the model.

Press reaction to the model was very much more restrained than it had been in America. This was largely because the 240Z was not to be offered at the bargain prices which were to be found on the other side of the Atlantic. The reason for this was due simply to the very much higher cost of transportation between Japan and Britain than between Japan and America's West Coast. This resulted in the car's being compared not with MGBs and GT6s, but with the Porsche 911T, Mercedes 280SL, 4.2 E-Type Jaguar, Alfa Romeo 2000 GTV and Lotus Elan +2. Still, the Datsun acquitted itself very well in such company. *Autocar* magazine's test in May 1971 showed the 911 to be just 4mph faster, but fractionally slower on the 0 – 60 time. The 4.2 E-Type was 0.6 of a second faster than the 240Z on 0 – 60, and just 0.8 of a second faster over the quarter mile.

There were, however, areas of the Z's character which road testers were critical of. It was generally agreed that the seats were poorly padded, the low-speed ride was poor, the drive line was full of clonks and creaks, and the ventilation system should have been designed to allow cold air to the vents whilst warm air was being channelled to the feet. These criticisms were quite justified; these areas could certainly have been better, but none of them was serious enough to detract from an otherwise excellent package.

Due to the different price bracket in which the 240Z was competing, the sales performance was somewhat limited. Sources indicate that 1970 saw only two official imports. These were

doubtless only for publicity purposes as customer cars were not generally available until mid-1971. Sales were rather slow; only 72 cars being sold in 1971. This picked up considerably to 602 for 1972 as the virtues of the new model started to become clear, and its rally successes provided the right rugged and sporting image. 1973, the last full year of 240Z sales, saw a further increase to 774.

For the home market Nissan had built a separate model, the Fairlady Z. It was outwardly the same as the 240Z but, due to Japan's tax laws favouring vehicles with engines of under 2-litre capacity, was offered with a 1998cc version of the 240Z's unit. A second version, known as the ZL, offered a higher trim package along with the five-speed gearbox and higher final drive ratio.

Sporting Success

Nissan had realised that a successful competition programme would be most valuable in building their international sales. To this end the developed yet another model to be available only to the home market. This was the Z432. Outwardly distinguishable only by its badging, twin tail pipes and magnesium wheels, the 432 boasted an entirely different engine (also a 2-litre six-cylinder) to the normal L series unit. This engine, designated the S20, was of 1989cc, with twin overhead cams, three solex twin-choke carbs and four valves per cylinder. Power output was put at 160bhp, being the most powerful of the early Z's. The 432 was moderately successful, winning local events.

Nissan's international plans for sporting honours with the Z432 were knocked on the head by the efforts of American Peter Brock's BRE Team. They had run a works-backed team with the SR311 Fairlady 2000 and, quite

naturally, Nissan provided them with a couple of 240Zs, even before it was announced, for racing development.

Brock Racing Enterprises intended to run the Z in the Sports Car Club of America C-production class and, as this class was only open to cars on sale in the States, they were unable to use the Z432. So Brock started some serious development of the 240 engine. They were soon running into serious problems with crank vibration and this led to the car's retiring from its first race, whilst leading, when the clutch vibrated apart.

Fortunately, Nissan were aware of the crank weakness, but the Brock team couldn't wait while Nissan put the redesigned crank into production, so they cobbled up a clutch which would withstand the vibration and, with this, the team scored its first win. Meanwhile, Brock's engineers were modifying the cranks and achieved considerable improvements. Finally the new cranks arrived from the factory, and the team never looked back. They were soon building 280bhp engines which would run to 8000rpm and sent one of these units to the Nissan High Performance Department in Japan, where they were working on the development of the Z432 engine. Once they had evaluated the Brock engine, and had had a chance to take in their findings, the S20 twin cam unit's development ground to a halt, but not before it had powered Z432s to victory in Eastern events. During 1971 Z-cars won at the Japanese Grand Prix, the Selangor Grand Prix and the Singapore Grand Prix (GT class). The Brock Team's 240Z won the SCCA Championship in its first year, and went on to repeat the achievement the following year, driven through both seasons by John Morton.

The BRE Team was disbanded the next year, leaving the other major Z team, Bob Sharp Racing, which had won the SCCA North Eastern Division title in 1971, to take the 1972 National title. Bob Sharp, driving his own car, won again in 1973.

1974 saw the introduction of the 260Z, and Walt Maas took his example to SCCA Championship victory, followed in 1975 by Bob Sharp, this time in the 280Z.

This run of Championships continued with Elliot Forbes-Robinson (1976), Logan Blackburn (1977) and Frank Leary (1978), all in 280Zs, to complete a 100 per cent success rate over nine years of SCCA titles!

On the UK scene, the Z was not to have such a series of runaway successes, the greatest claim to fame being the Samuri Motor Company's hard-fought win in the 1974 RAC 'Modsports' Championship. The Samuri Company had been started a couple of years earlier when the founder, Spike Anderson, an ex-Broadspeed cylinder head man, had bought a brand new 240Z, Reg. No. FFA 196L. He was soon looking for more power, and modified the engine by gas-flowing the head and fitting triple Weber 40 DCOE carbs along with a fabricated six-branch exhaust manifold. The now famous Samuri paint job was added. Motoring journalist Clive Richardson was invited to test it and, on the eve of the test when the final touches were being added, someone asked, 'What are you going to call it?' Various names were thrown around until 'Samurai' was settled on as a choice, and the signwriter, who had just painted the coach striping, was asked to paint on the new name. The problem was that nobody was sure how to spell Samurai. The consensus was that SAMURI was correct, so this was how it was painted!

The road test and resulting article were a great success and, over the next six years or so, led to Spike's producing some 74 full 'Super Samuris' (which included

the special paint) to various specifications as required by the individual customers, as well as numerous less comprehensive conversions. A full reprint of a road test on Spike's own Super Samuri appears later in the book.

It was following a track test to establish the success of a ventilated disc and four-pot caliper brake conversion (which was being observed by Automotive Products, who had supplied the hardwear), that the idea of building a full house racer came up. Enter Bob Gathercole, Spike's new partner, with the ex-Rauno Aaltonen 1970 works rally car, a road test of which is featured further on.

This was converted into a full racer and named 'Big Sam'. Following a battle of Olympian magnitude, which included a couple of engine failures and a very heavy accident which wrote off the body shell, driver Win Percy took Big Sam to championship victory from several quick 3-litre Porsche Carreras by just one point.

For the international rally scene Nissan's aims were to win with the 240Z two major rallies which were the antithesis of each other: the Monte Carlo and the East African Safari.

It was obviously out of the question for the 240Z to be ready for the 1970 Safari, so the 510 Bluebird 1600SSS was used to good effect by Edgar Herrmann, who gave Nissan their first Safari win. Development of the new model was under way, however, as both Rauno Aaltonen and Tony Fall had been co-opted immediately after the 1970 Monte to carry out testing over the Monte route. By the time the cars appeared in their first International, the 1970 RAC, they had been made very competitive. Five works cars were imported, four finally taking part in the 2300-mile forest event. Their run was to be troubled from early on by differential failures but, in spite of the resulting penalties, Aaltonen

brought his car in a creditable seventh and established the 240Z as a firm favourite with the huge number of spectators present.

While the RAC was in progress the team back in Japan were preparing another group of 240Zs for the '71 Monte. Again Aaltonen headed the team by finishing fifth.

Possibly the most important event for the team was the 1971 Safari where four cars were entered. In total, 107 cars were flagged off on 8 April from the Nairobi start by Kenya's President Jomo Kenyatta, for a 6300km odyssey around East Africa. By the time the crews reached Mombasa, Aaltonen and Easter were leading the rally, followed closely by other works cars from Porsche, Lancia and Ford.

They were soon in trouble, though, with broken suspension following a collision with a rock. By the end of the first leg Waldegaard's 911S was leading, followed in second and third places by Herrmann and Aaltonen. Shekhar Mehta and Mike Doughty, driving the third of the surviving Datsuns, were lying sixth. On the final leg, a battle royal developed between the Datsun and Porsche teams which was finally resolved in favour of the Japanese with Herrmann and Schuller winning by just three points from team-mates Mehta and Doughty. Aaltonen and Easter finished seventh to ensure that Nissan also took the team prize.

1971 also saw the 240Z's first victory in Europe when Tony Fall won the Welsh Rally, but later that year on the RAC the best the team could manage was nineteenth.

Having won the Safari in 1970 and 1971, Nissan were obviously keen on making it a hat trick and so for the 1972 event they paired Aaltonen and Fall in the same car. The theory was that two top class all-rounders would have a strong advantage over other crews whose drivers would have little opportunity to rest. The plan collapsed due to clutch failure and the three car team came in fifth, sixth and tenth.

Other events that year were more successful; Aaltonen managed a superb third on the Monte, his car fitted with a 255bhp, 2498cc, cross-flow-headed, fuel-injected engine. Victories on the Montana Rally of Portugal and the Kenya 2000 Rally followed and the team were unlucky when Aaltonen, co-driven by local man Steve Halloran, was relegated to second on the Australian Southern Cross Rally on a technicality, having won the event on the road. Tony Fall finished the TAP Rally in fourth place and Shekhar Mehta managed sixth on the Acropolis.

The team's achievements with the 240Z continued in 1973 with a second victory on the Safari, this time for Mehta after Aaltonen had rolled whilst leading, and a good win on the Tanzania 1000 Rally. Alas, ninth was the best that could be mustered on the Monte and, as this was the factory's last season with the 240Z, they were to fail in their ambition. For the '74 season the team started with the 260Z, but a major policy decision resulted in the team switching to the Violet saloon, so the 260Z was used only on the Safari where Harry Kallstrom finished fourth and the second works car fifth. This was the end of the Z's official rallying life, but privateers, many with ex-works cars, continued to campaign their vehicles. Down under in Australia Ross Dunkerton

won the Australian Rally Championship in 1975, '76 and '77. Several works cars remained in Britain and one, supported by Old Woking Service Station, who hosted the official Datsun team, and driven by Kevin Videan, finished second in the 1975 *Motoring News* Road Rally Championship. The car in which Tony Fall won the Welsh Rally was sold to Withers of Winsford who ran it under two different registration numbers for both Chris Sclater and Roy Fidler on UK National as well as International events. A couple of cars went to Portugal and it was one of these, driven by Antonio Carlos de Oliveira which won the 1972 Rally of the Camellias. Old Woking Service Station retained a late cross-flow car and both Mehta and works co-driver Schuller retained cars.

All things considered, the Z had a most remarkable sporting history, its exceptional ruggedness being put to good use on those

rallies where endurance was a critical factor. On European sprint events it was less successful as the homologation specials were starting to take over, leaving little space for a genuine production car to shine. It was, however, a great success with the spectators who loved its noise and sideways style so much that the publicity value was very often greater for Datsun than for a winning car which usually lacked the Z's character. The Z will always be remembered for that.

EVOLUTION

Datsun chose the Tokyo Motor Show of November 1969 to launch the 240Z, and in only a few months the first production cars were arriving in the States. The body/chassis unit was of monocoque construction, a pure two-seater with strong lines and perfect balance. It was just right from stem to stern; crisp, clean, aggressive and masculine. Ally that to the performance and handling and you have an exceptional motor car. But there is one other vital ingredient required – character – and that the Z simply oozed.

Many of the details of the new model had filtered through to the UK via American magazines prior to the British launch, but the first demonstrators to arrive in Britain had the addition of a five-speed gearbox which was only an option in America. The emission equipment was not fitted and the radio/electric aerial was listed as an option as was the heated rear window, which rapidly became standard!

When the first production vehicles started to filter through in the spring of 1971 there were many detail differences, not only compared with the American models, but comparing different UK cars! By late summer, however, the variations started to settle down and the basic UK specification emerged, but the model was always subject to inexplicable detail differences, one specialist saying, to this day, 'I have never seen two cars the same!'

Some examples had front and rear over-riders, others front only and others rear only. Number plate lights were either above the number plate (plastic) as US cars, or mounted on the top of the bumper (chrome). Fuel filler flaps came with locks, or turn knobs, or were simply held shut by a spring.

The first few UK cars arrived with the front indicators/side lights mounted on the front valances as the American cars had. Datsun had both amber and white lenses available, but neither would meet British legal requirements as neither orange side lights nor white indicators were legal. To add to the problem the lights were below the legal minimum height. To meet these requirements the British models started to arrive minus the offending lamps but with the addition of separate indicators mounted on top of the bumper. This, according to one dealer, was not the end of the story as these cars were delivered without any side lights! Dealers were reputed to have changed the original headlights to ones incorporating side lights prior to the vehicles' being sold. This story is supported by the fact that the side light wiring was, to say the least, an amateur job on UK vehicles manufactured before 1972, and the lamps themselves were of Lucas manufacture, whereas the original specification listed Roito headlights.

Note the phrase above 'vehicles manufactured before 1972'. It is an interesting point that, due to the extended transportation time from Japan, specification changes took several months to filter into the showrooms and, consequently, it becomes difficult to say precisely when some specification changes came into being.

The first notable detail revisions were for the 1971 model year, and hence reached the showrooms around April, when the ventilation outlets were changed from rectangular slatted vents below the rear window. The new outlets were incorporated into the rear pillars, necessitating the discontinuation of the '240Z' badge and the addition of a combined circular 'Z' badge and outlet cover. This was also the point at which the UK cars acquired their spoilers as standard and the revised indicators/side lights previously mentioned. The hand throttle was removed, the cut-out for it being blanked off.

Significant changes in the 240Z's specification took place for the 1972 model year. The differential unit was moved rearward by 35mm to reduce the angle through which the driveshafts operated. This was accomplished by redesigning the subframe and lengthening the propshaft to suit. Modifications were also made to the centre console. All evidence of the hand throttle was done away with, the ashtray repositioned behind the gear lever, the cigar lighter was moved onto the dashboard and the heated rear window switch repositioned on the fuse box cover. Revised hub caps were fitted and these were destined to remain until the late seventies. All the vehicles built to 1971 specification were manufactured by the end of July.

The next set of changes was first seen in the showrooms around April 1972 having been produced from the beginning of January. These changes were far less obvious than those previously detailed, but equally important. The gearbox (five-speed) was changed from the FS5C71A to the FS5C71B (see *Buyer's Guide*) and the compression ratio was lowered by 0.2:1 to 8.8:1. In the UK, interior colour options were discontinued, black becoming standard. Most customers were happy about this as the other UK colours – tan and turquoise (!) – were generally unloved. In America, colour options continued to be available, including red and white in addition to those previously available in Britain. The elements of the heated rear window changed from vertical to horizontal and this became the easiest way to identify a car of pre-1972 manufacture. In the US, 5 inch rims became standard instead of optional, adding half an inch.

From March 1972 the factory started to fit a new propshaft to improve driveline smoothness; its mounting to the gearbox was by a bolt-on flange whereas previously it had been by sliding spline. The new propshaft featured a splined joint further along its length. These vehicles would have reached the showrooms around July.

Cars for the '73 model year were in manufacture from July onwards and improvements included a larger, $7^{1}/2$ inch servo (previously they had been 6 inches) and an intermittent wipe facility. The UK cars also received a throttle closure delay diaphragm which reduced the engine's responsiveness.

In America, increasingly stringent legal requirements resulted in some fairly drastic steps having to be taken in order to comply, and during 1973 the carburettors and inlet and exhaust manifolds had to be changed to include gas recirculation. Bumpers and mountings were revised and strengthened and larger, strong over-riders were fitted adding 6 inches to the car's length. The resulting weight increases and power losses reduced the model's appeal, but Datsun had a trick up their sleeve – the 260Z. The last 240Z came off the production line at the end of July 1973, the 260Z going straight into production for 1974 delivery.

260Z

Outwardly the new model was little different from that which it replaced but, both mechanically and internally, there were many changes. The most obvious was the revised engine size, brought about by increasing the stroke by 5.3mm to 79mm resulting in a capacity of 2565cc. All markets now received the new carburettors and manifolds, and in America electronic ignition was featured. The result was a fairly substantial increase in power and torque, but the longer stroke and revised breathing reduced the engine's willingness to rev. Revision of the gear ratios and a change (on five-speed models) in the final drive ratio from 3.9:1 to 3.7:1 resulted in the UK 260Z's performance being only slightly down on the early 240Z. In America the picture was different. The extensive crash and emission control equipment resulted in the 260Z's performance falling almost exactly between the first and last 240Z. From the chassis point of view, detail changes were made to the shock absorbers, and the spring rates were increased to counter the extra weight. The US models received the rear anti-roll bars which most other markets had had on the 240Z.

On the interior side, flame-resistant materials were employed, and all the trim was tidied up. The heater controls were revised and two rectangular fresh air vents replaced the 240's much smaller central fascia outlet. A heavy looking vinyl-covered steering wheel replaced the 'wood-rim'. The British version continued to have a black only interior, while the Americans had a choice of black, tan, off-white and dark brown. Other options for the US market included three-speed automatic and four- or five-speed manual transmissions, along with air conditioning, all of which had been available on the now defunct 240Z.

Externally the only changes were confined to badges, a revised rear panel and lights which separated the reversing lamps from the main cluster, moving them inwards. A second gas-filled strut was employed to assist tailgate opening.

In October 1973, the 260Z 2+2 went into production for launching in early 1974 (March in the case of the UK). The extra space required was obtained by increasing the wheelbase by 11.9 inches, revising the roofline and enlarging the doors to allow easier access. Mechanically it was virtually identical to the two-seater, but featured a still larger servo and, on the European models, still harder springs to counter the extra weight.

In the US the 260Z was to have a run of little over a year and, during that time, the only significant change was the addition of huge 'federal' bumpers, which were to be featured on the new model for 1975, the 280Z.

280Z

The extra capacity was achieved by increasing the bore to 86mm giving a capacity of 2754cc. Probably more important, however, was the addition of licence-made Bosch L Jetronic fuel injection. This cured problems with the rather unsatisfactory 260Z carbs, improving performance and economy, and keeping exhaust emissions within legal limits.

There were, of course, other changes in the new model, including a lower compression ratio achieved by revisions to the combustion chambers, larger valves and ports, 195/70 HR-14 tyres, new gear and final drive ratios, increased spring rates (yet again), carpet to the transmission tunnel and rear inner wheel arches to replace the quilted vinyl, larger fuel tank, new front indicators, and much more besides.

Meanwhile, in the rest of the world, the 260Z was being sold, but UK sales were down and, for 1976, the two-seater was dropped, to return for 1977. By now the 260Z had inherited the final drive and new five-speed gearbox that were being fitted to the 280Z for 1977, along with alloy wheels and 195/70 tyres.

In addition to the new 'box, the 280Z received an AM/FM radio with eight-track stereo, new wheel trims, a collapsible spare tyre, and bonnet vents which replaced the front wing flaps of the earlier models.

The evolution of the Z cars was now complete as, midway through 1978, they were replaced by the all-new-bodyshelled 280ZX. During the Z's eight year reign, over half a million examples were sold, more than any other sportscar in the history of motoring.

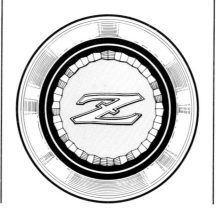

SPECIFICATION

Datsun 240Z, 260Z and 280Z

Type Designation **Built**	S30 Nissan Motors, Tokyo, Japan TOTAL BUILT: 542,208
Engine	Front-mounted, cast-iron block, in line six-cylinder, seven main bearing crank, aluminium cylinder head housing chain-driven single overhead camshaft.
Transmission	Front-mounted four- or five-speed all-synchromesh gearbox driving through single dry-plate diaphragm clutch or three-speed Jatco automatic gearbox and torque converter to rear wheels via hypoid bevel chassis-mounted differential.
Chassis	Unitary constructed body/chassis unit – all steel. Front crossmember providing engine and suspension mountings. Rear subframe providing differential and rear suspension mountings.
Suspension/Steering	Independent by MacPherson struts, coil springs, telescopic dampers and anti-roll bars with front radius rods and rear lower wishbones. Rack and pinion steering of 2.7 turns lock-to-lock.
Brakes	Dual circuit hydraulic with servo assistance. Front 10.67 inch discs with two piston calipers. Rear 9 inch aluminium finned drums. Cable operated handbrake.
Electrical System	12 volt negative earth. 50 amp/hour battery, Hitachi alternator of 37.5 or 45 amp depending on market, Hitachi pre-engaged starter motor.

Power Output, Performance & Gearing

Model	240Z	240Z	240Z	240Z
Gearbox	4 SP	Auto	5 SP	4 SP
Market	US	US	UK	US
Year	1970	1971	1972	1973
Compression ratio	9.0	9.0	9.0	8.8
BHP @ RPM	151/5600	150/6000	151/5600	129/6000
Torque @ RPM	146/4400	146/4400	146/4400	127/4400

Power measurement	SAE gross	SAE gross	SAE gross	SAE nett
0–60 mph	7.8	10.4	8.0	11.9
0–100 mph	22.8	32.5	24.0	33.5
Standing 1/4 mile	16.1	17.6	15.8	18.6
Max speed				
1st	42	55	40	40
2nd	68	90	65	65
3rd	105	120	90	103
4th	122	N/A	120	115
5th	N/A	N/A	125	N/A
Weight, lb	2330	2405	2284	2450
Gear ratios:				
1st	3.549	2.458	2.957	3.549
2nd	2.197	1.458	1.857	2.197
3rd	1.415	1.00	1.311	1.415
4th	1.00	N/A	1.00	1.00
5th	N/A	N/A	0.852	N/A
Overall ratios:				
1st	11.92	8.71	11.53	11.92
2nd	7.39	5.17	7.24	7.39
3rd	4.77	3.54	5.11	4.77
4th	3.36	N/A	3.90	3.36
5th	N/A	N/A	3.32	N/A
Final drive	3.364	3.54	3.90	3.364

Model	260 Z	260 Z 2+2	260 Z 2+2	260 Z	260 Z	280 Z
Gearbox	4 SP	4 SP	5 SP	5 SP	5 SP	4(5) SP
Market	US CAL	US	UK	UK	UK	US
Year	1974	1974	1974	1975	1977	1977
Compression ratio	8.8	8.8	8.3	8.3	9.2	8.3
BHP @ RRM	139/5200	139/5200	150/5400	162/5600	150/5400	170/5600
Torque @ RPM	137/4400	137/4400	158/4400	152/4400	158/4400	177/4400
Power measurement	SAE nett	SAE nett	DIN nett	SAE gross	DIN nett	SAE gross
0–60 mph	9.9	11.6	9.9	8.2	10.2	9.4
0–100 mph	35.8	35	31.1	23.8	33.5	30.2
Standing 1/4 mile	17.3	17.3	17.3	15.7	17.0	17.3
Max speed:						
1st	37	40	46	43	44	41
2nd	60	64	69	65	66	67
3rd	96	81	101	96	94	104
4th	116	115	115	125	112	119
5th	N/A	N/A	120	127	115	(-)
Weight lb	2665	2750	2630	2425	2548	2875
Gear ratios:						
1st	3.592	3.592	2.906	2.906	3.32	3.32
2nd	2.246	2.246	1.902	1.902	2.08	2.08
3rd	1.415	1.415	1.308	1.308	1.311	1.311
4th	1.00	1.00	1.00	1.00	1.00	1.00
5th	N/A	N/A	0.864	0.864	0.864	(0.864)
Overall ratios:						
1st	12.07	12.07	10.75	10.75	11.79	11.79
2nd	7.55	7.55	7.04	7.04	7.38	7.38
3rd	4.75	4.75	4.84	4.84	4.65	4.65
4th	3.36	3.36	3.70	3.70	3.55	3.55
5th	N/A	N/A	3.19	3.19	3.06	(3.06)
Final drive	3.364	3.364	3.70	3.70	3.55	3.55

Engine Types & Dimensions

Model	Fairlady Z	Fairlady Z432	240Z	260Z	280Z
Engine type	L20	S20	L24	L26	L28
Bore mm/in	70/2.75	82/3.23	83/3.27	83/3.27	86/3.39
Stroke mm/in	69.7/2.74	62.8/2.47	73.7/2.9	79/3.11	79/3.11
Capacity cc/cu in	1998/121.9	1989/121.4	2393/146	2565/156.8	2754/168
Manf. Date	1969-1978	1969-1973	1969-1973	1973-1978	1975-1978
Quantity built	75216	419	156076	80369	230128
Carbs/Injection	2 x SU	3 x Solex	2 x SU	2 x SU	Bosch EFI

Dimensions

	2-Seaters	2+2-Seaters
Front track	4ft 5^1/$_2$in/136cm	4ft 5^1/$_2$in/136cm
Rear track	4ft 5in/135cm	4ft 5in/135cm
Wheelbase	7ft 6^1/$_2$in/200cm	8ft 6^1/$_2$in/230.5cm
Width	5ft 4in/162.5cm	5ft 5in/165cm
Height	4ft 2^3/$_4$in/129cm	4ft 2^2/$_3$in/129cm

Overall length:

240Z, 260Z	13ft 5in (no over-riders)
240Z	13ft 8in (over-riders)
Late 240Z, 260Z US	14ft 1in
280Z	14ft 5in
260Z 2+2	14ft 6in
260Z 2+2, 280Z 2+2 US	15ft 1in

C1

C1. In 1972 Japan was offered the 240Z. With it came the ZG, a long-nosed, aerodynamic version. The longer front panels and wheel arch extensions were all fibreglass and made the car some 7½ inches longer. The headlamp scoops were closed in by transparent cowls. A few of these models filtered through to England.

C2. The Fairlady Z432 engine bay. This unit, designated S20, was a detuned version of the R380 sports racing car's engine. Note the criss-cross radiator grille common to other Japanese specification Zs, and the radiator cap security chain.

C2

C3

C3. Full frontal. Perhaps the Z's prettiest view.

C4. Shades of GTO Ferrari. The beautifully sleek profile common to all two-seater Zs.

C5. The standard UK specification 240Z engine. This one is of late '71 manufacture. Note the underbonnet lamp at the bottom of the picture. Several feet of cable are stored within to allow it to reach any part of the engine bay.

C5

C4

C6

C7

C8   C9

C6. Mike Feeney's tastefully customised Chevrolet V8 converted 240Z features amongst its comprehensive specification Jaguar rear suspension and limited slip differential.

C7. John Toms' immaculate 1971 240Z fitted, as many have been, with Wolfrace wheels. John has owned this car from new.

C8. Here are two unique Zs; the registration numbers, which are quite genuine, are of Irish origin. '240Z' is owned by Margaret Bukowski and '260Z' by Graham Miller.

C9. The basic interior layout of the Z series remained virtually unchanged during its production life. This is a 1972 240Z.

C10

C11

C12

C10. The most substantial dash changes took place on the centre console to the heater controls and ventilation outlets. This is an American specification 280Z which featured additional detail changes.

C11. Compare the profile of the 260Z 2 + 2 with the 240Z reproduced elsewhere. When a manufacturer produces a 2 + 2 version of a two-seater model, the overall shape is often unbalanced. The Z worked much better and many find the 2 + 2's extra length and longer roofline actually improves the shape.

C12. Aggressive frontal view of a 260Z which, from this angle, is indistinguishable from a 240Z. This shot shows the standard rubber front spoiler very well. Owner Allan Exley has blacked out all the bright work on this car.

C13

C14

C13. *This 240Z, in one of the most attractive colours offered, features the 260Z alloy wheels.*

C14. *The Z Club's Chairman, Lynne Godber, keeps her 1971 240Z in mint condition. It is the only known UK car still retaining the early hubcaps.*

C15. *This 260Z 2 + 2 features wind deflectors to help clear the rear window. It would have been a good idea for Datsun to offer a rear wiper as an option.*

C15

C16

C17

C16. An unusually late and very original 240Z flanks an equally original-looking 260Z 2 + 2.

C17. Magnificent Seven!

C18. Moral victors of the 1972 Australian Southern Cross Rally were Rauno Aaltonen and Steve Halloran, who were relegated to second following a minor infringement of the rules regarding advertising on the vehicle.

C19. Datsun's Safari victory with the 240Z on the '71 event was followed by a poor showing in '72. Datsun was once again on the winner's rostrum in 1973, however, when Shehkar Mehta/Lofty Drews brought car No. 1 in first.

C20. The 260Z was used on the Safari by the works team in 1974, its only official showing. This shot shows Harry Kallstrom's 260Z on its way to 4th overall. Another 260Z, driven by Tanzanian Zully Remtulla, came in 5th.

C18

C19

C20

C21. The works car of Tony Fall/Mike Wood slides gently through a hairpin during the 1973 Monte Carlo Rally. The Monte cars all had the faired-in headlights.

C22. A privately-entered 240Z ploughs through the mud in a very wet section of the 1973 East African Safari.

AUTOCAR 10 December 1970

Given the Works:

DATSUN 240Z

ROAD TESTS

Driving Rauno Aaltonen's RAC Rally car; a first look at this exciting Japanese GT

By Ray Hutton

THE news, when published earlier this year, that Datsun were again to take part in the RAC Rally came as no surprise. In 1969 they had taken the team award with three 1600SSS saloons. Since then they had turned a 1969 team prize in the East African Safari into a win in the 1970 event and they clearly had hopes of a similar progression in the forests of Britain. What *did* surprise us was that the cars they entered were the new 240Z sports coupés, a model which, until this year's London Motor Show, had never been seen in England.

The Datsun 240Z was announced 12 months before at the Tokyo Motor Show and imports to the United States (at which market it is obviously primarily aimed) started early this year. Judging by the rave reviews it has received in the American enthusiast Press, it is a big success there and a few examples have already run in SCCA production car racing. The model has hardly been seen in Europe, and it has not yet been decided if it is to be marketed in Britain.

Datsun's RAC Rally effort should be an object lesson to some European manufacturers.

Early in October, five rally-prepared 240Zs arrived in England for what was to be their first international event. Prepared to Group 3 (the RAC does not allow prototypes), they were equipped with modified engines, suitable gearing, lightweight panels and a whole string of special items. Engineer Takashi Wakabayashi and his team in Nissan's engineering laboratories had done a very thorough job to develop and get all these bits and pieces through the complex procedure of homologation (despite virtually no competition experience with the model) before the company's rally plans were made public.

To ensure that thorough preparation was carried through with the same professional approach, they enlisted top drivers Rauno Aaltonen (who had driven a 1600SSS in the 1969 RAC), Tony Fall and their Safari winner Edgar Hermann. A fourth, spare car was an additional last-minute entry for 1969 RAC Rally Champion John Bloxham. The fifth 240Z was used as a service car (taking a leaf out of Porsche's book, who use 0911s as high speed tenders) and joined the service vehicles

Performance Check

Maximum speeds

Gear	Top	4th	3rd	2nd	1st
mph	126*	112	84	60	36

Acceleration*

mph	30	40	50	60	70	80	90	100	110
sec	4.1	5.4	7.1	9.0	10.6	12.6	16.2	18.8	25.6

Standing ¼ mile: 16.0sec 89mph
Standing Kilometre: 27.5sec 117mph
*see text

Super Profile

operated by two mechanics from Japan and staff from Old Woking Service Station, the British base for the operation.

Aaltonen had carried out some testing with the model just after this year's Monte Carlo Rally and did a couple of days' rough road testing at Bagshot in the weeks preceding the RAC, while Tony Fall used his car in a British club event to acclimitize himself. Initial impressions of these big (by rally standards), brutish cars seemed to suggest that they were going to be quite a handful—one driver said that it was like an Austin Healey 3000 "before sorting".

Differentials spoil chances

The four-strong team of red and black 240Zs were together with the French Alpines (also making their first British appearance) the centre of attraction at the start of the Rally. Tony Fall, enjoying himself hugely, was well-placed in the early stages but became involved with Ove Andersson's already-spun Alpine on the Dalby South stage in Yorkshire on the first night and

The engine is a large lump for a 2.4 litre unit. The three carburettors are Japanese-made Solex. Access to the washer bottle and battery in the back corners of the bonnet is via small flaps on top of the wings.

A comfortable interior with well-planned controls but some lack of stowage space for odd essential items. The special seats are non-reclining; Willans full harnesses are fitted. Note the high windscreen washer post on the scuttle

though he continued, retired on the next stage with a broken differential. Rauno Aaltonen had transmission trouble early on, when a drive-shaft broke on the first of the Clipstone stages. He thought at first that a tyre had punctured and drove to the end of the stage, where the broken drive-shaft and the brake pipes and cables it had damaged while flailing around were discovered. He and Easter removed the shaft and drove the next stage with one only (and no rear brakes) to reach their service crew, who fitted a shaft from their Datsun 1800. The brakes were progressively repaired by service crews throughout the night, but it was not until Bathgate control on the Sunday morning that the car's full braking was restored. On the return from the Scottish loop this car also suffered differential failure; fortunately they were able to get to the control and the unit was changed. Thereafter this car ran beautifully and steadily improved its position. In the latter stages it proved as fast as the quickest of the opposition, particularly on the faster stages; Aaltonen set fastest time on three stages and finished a strong seventh; he would

The 240Z is the first serious attempt to rally a big-rorty-front-engined sports car since the Austin Healey 3000. Aaltonen's car remained remarkably unblemished after 2,300 miles of RAC Rally

The doors and the bonnet are made of glass-fibre with plastic windows and the tailgate is so thin that it has a noticeable droop when supported open. Note the mud-flaps, mounted well back

clearly have been much better placed had he not lost so much time early on. We had particular reason to be hopeful that this car would finish, for it was agreed that we could borrow it for the weekend after the rally had ended.

The two other team cars were victims of the same differential trouble; Datsun were by no means alone in this, for transmission failure was the universal cause of the mechanical retirements that affected the works teams.

First close look

Our weekend with number 18, the Aaltonen-Easter car, provided an opportunity not only to drive what is already a highly competitive rally car but also our first chance to examine the model in detail. Driving specially prepared competition cars is always an interesting exercise, and never more so than this, but it was curious to have no reference point by which to judge its performance and behaviour; none of us has driven a standard 240Z.

As it is so new to us, a run through the standard car's specification is perhaps appropriate. The 240Z is a front engine-rear drive coupé powered by a bulky in-line six-cylinder overhead camshaft engine of 2,393 c.c. which is, in effect, the familiar 1600 c.c. engine with two extra cylinders. It has bore and stroke measurements of 83mm x 73.3mm and produces 150 bhp (gross) at 5,600 rpm. It is available with either a four- or five-speed gearbox, has MacPherson strut and trailing link front suspension and an independent rear end, using struts again with lower wishbones. Rack and pinion steering and a mixed disc-drum brake set-up are employed. The two-seater steel coupé body has bits of several different cars in its styling (influences of the Jaguar E-type, Toyota 2000GT and several Ferraris are evident) but the overall effect is sporting, eye-catching and pleasing. A criticism might be its height off the ground—a feature which is of course of distinct advantage for rough-road rallying.

Exact details of all the internal modifications carried out in the preparation of the rally cars unfortunately are not available. The work was done in Japan and with characteristic inscrutability it was explained to us that the car was "fairly standard". The engine, which is normally equipped with two SU-type Hitachi carburettors, is fitted with three Mikuni-Solex twin-choke instruments and with a different camshaft; power has been increased to a quoted figure of 200 bhp (net). The gearbox, the five-speed version of course, has been re-ratioed and an ultra-low 4.87 final drive fitted (standard cars have a 3.9 axle; those sold in the US, 3.36). The limited-slip differentials, which proved the model's weakest link, had all suffered from loosening or breakage of the crown wheel bolts, not specifically from over-heating (as was suspected at the time). Aaltonen had been worried as to whether the renewed diff on his car would last, and we were worried too, since it made dreadful sounds like broken glass when the car was reversed. Incidentally, though the Datsun's US options list includes a clutch-type limited-slip differential, this one had the characteristics of the cam-and-plunger type.

A glance underneath the car, to examine the cause of a slight but audible movement at one of the mounting points of the sub-frame that carries the differential, suggested that very little underbody strengthening had been necessary. There is the usual front undershield (rather more than a sump guard) but otherwise it really did seem "fairly standard" and it is a credit to the car's strength that it survived 2,300 miles of RAC Rally without any apparent damage. The wheels fitted are Datsun magnesium alloy designs; 14in. diameter with 6in. wide rims.

AUTOCAR 10 December 1970

GIVEN THE WORKS:
DATSUN 240Z . . .

Lightweight glass-fibre panels replace the doors, the bonnet and opening tailgate, and all side and rear windows are plastic. Outwardly the body changes are few—two strengthened jacking points at the sides, Safari-style mudflaps and a row of four modest-looking but highly effective Japanese supplementary lamps firmly outrigged in what seems a very damage-prone position. The standard bumpers remain. Oh, and there's two enormous megaphoned exhaust pipes.

No 18 on the road

Those exhausts give advance warning of the sort of noise the beast makes when it is fired up. The noise is "very considerable", absolutely glorious and of questionable legality when the engine is on song—the noise guessing game of "who comes next" on the stages of the RAC provided a lot of Datsuns mistaken for Porsches. Actual starting up (on the key) is no problem at all and is preceded by a subdued clatter from the electric fuel pump behind you (colleague Michael Scarlett insists that it be likened to a covey of ladies from a Japanese Womens' Institute all knitting furiously). Surprisingly, the engine will idle quite happily at 800 rpm. Moving off, gently, is no problem either; the clutch is not unduly heavy (though of the competition variety) and the engine remarkably tractable. The transition when the road clears and the throttles are opened is an experience of a very special kind—the harsh, raucous exhaust note is directly proportional to the rate at which the revs rise, almost as if the accelerator was a volume control. There is a leap forward after 3,500 rpm but the engine is not "cammy" in the racing sense, just beautifully responsive throughout. And it will pull in 5th gear from 1,100 rpm. Noise level towards maximum revs of 6,800 is too high for normal conversation—hence the inevitable intercom.

The gearbox, all-synchromesh and with its five speeds arranged Alfa Romeo-style (1st to 4th in the standard positions, 5th to the right of 3rd, above reverse) is one of the best five-speeders we have tried.

With the gearing arranged for short bursts between corners in the forests, we expected the acceleration to be impressive. Our figures show that it was (the 0-100 mph and standing quarter mile are closely comparable with those for a standard 4.2 Jaguar E-type) and they could certainly have been improved upon had we not felt inhibited by the sub-standard differential and tempered by our desire to return the car in running order. A gentle 3,000 rpm was used for our careful take-offs from rest (which gave just a touch of wheelspin) and 6,500 rpm in the gears. Serious vibration from the rear (the same diff trouble) prevented an accurate maximum speed run, but with such a low axle ratio the theoretical maximum of 126 mph is obviously realistic. For the record, the speedometer (in mph) was dead accurate, before its cable broke. A run of some 400 miles allowed a check on fuel consumption, which came out at 20.3 mpg, only slightly less than figures obtained for the standard car by our American contemporaries.

How it handles

The car came to us exactly as it had finished the rally, numbers, mud and all. It was fitted with German-made Dunlop SP 215/70 SR14 radials which were used in the later stages, though the cars started the rally on some Japanese Dunlops not unlike the Dunlop "Hakka" snow tyre though with a harder compound, which were said to be excellent on dry, rough roads. Traction on tarmac on these big "chunkies" was excellent and directional stability good. Under smooth road conditions, understeer was moderate and power-induced rear-end breakaway easy to obtain and easy to catch, but on slippery corners the works drivers' reports of excessive understeer were confirmed, the front end "ploughing" out, even without a burst of power. But by "setting up" the car in the right gear with power to spare, cornering could be rapid indeed and the power was planted on the road to a surprisingly high degree. Under forestry conditions Aaltonen was using the handbrake to do this; hence his

slower stage times when the rear brakes were not fully operative following the drive-shaft failure.

The car's braking performance had remained good, if noisy and harsh at low speed and requiring a firm push. The steering is only moderately heavy, nicely geared (2.6 turns from lock to lock) and responsive. The dampers had also stood up well to the long pounding and the ride is very reasonable—if sharp over the bigger bumps. The works drivers expressed enthusiasm for the car's performance over "yumps" and the lack of drama on landing. Overall, we were most impressed by the 240Z's feeling of solidity but it seems a big and hairy lump of car to hurl through the forests (perhaps that is its only real similarity to the Healey) and we are once again filled with admiration for those who are able to do so at stage-winning speeds.

Both the driver and navigator are well catered for in the cockpit. Special cloth-covered seats are fitted; the passenger sits lower than the driver because Rauno is short and likes to sit high, but none the less the driving position proved comfortable even for our largest tester. The steering wheel is a comfortable, fat, leather-rimmed affair, while the pedals have been arranged for "proper" heel-and-toeing and a clutch footrest added. The handbrake, floor-mounted, is of the fly-off type. Visibility to the front is fine, though one is conscious of there being rather more of the long bonnet than is visible and of the heavy screen pillars. To the rear and at the rear three-quarters, the view is obstructed by the bodywork and also by the hefty four-strut roll-over bar and two spare wheels. This essential 'luggage' restricts interior storage space considerably.

Well-planned controls

The standard dashboard layout has an American flavour, with deeply recessed dials. The dominant instruments are the paired speedometer and rev-counter, the three smaller dials at the centre showing water temperature and oil pressure (a source of some concern to us as it was never much over 30 psi), amps and fuel level, and the time, respectively. All normal lighting and wiper-washer operations are contained on a multiple stalk to the left of the steering column and the indicator stalk to the right, while the auxiliary lamps are looked after by an extra panel of six switches above (and obstructing) the heater-ventilator controls. Two separate Halda Tripmasters are fitted instead of the more usual Twinmaster; a fail-safe operation, since they are driven independently from the two front wheels.

As always, it is the details that are so fascinating—the separate flexible-stalk blue lights that illuminate the Haldas, the map light on the door, the intercom amplifier mounted on the roll-over bar, the passenger's floor button for the air-horns, the pockets, the Velcro-attached pads to prevent chafing knees on window winders, the multiplicity of straps to hold down wheels, tools and all manner of things in the back, and the sticky tape everywhere to hold spare fuses, keys and padding in place—and even to show the driver where dead centre on the steering wheel is.

It is things like this that make rally cars so different from the standard article. This Datsun 240Z, which impressed us tremendously, could be a very different kettle of fish from the standard car. But if the "cooking" version shows only a percentage of the flair of this car, we await its introduction to Britain (which must surely come) with eager anticipation. In the meantime, Datsun intend to follow up their promising rally debut with a full programme of events next year, starting off with the Monte, when their drivers will once again be Rauno Aaltonen and Tony Fall.

Not us—but the Little Finn himself, hurling the 240Z through the Grizedale stage on the RAC. Aaltonen finished seventh—one place better than he managed in 1969 with the Datsun 1600SSS saloon

Super Profile

Road test/John Bolster

Datsun 240Z: A sports car for enjoyment

The 240Z, a two-seater coupé of sporting appearance, makes a refreshing change from many sports cars.

Most sports cars are treated as poor relations and have to use components which are well enough for family saloons but were not tailored for the job. The Datsun 240 Z makes a refreshing change for it has a really close-ratio five-speed gearbox, high-geared steering, independent rear suspension, and a body which shares no panels with bread-and-butter models.

The car is a two-seater coupé of sporting appearance, having a lot of interior space for the two occupants and a vast luggage compartment, with straps attached to secure suitcases. The suspension is by MacPherson struts all round, with disc front and drum rear brakes, the servo furnishing only moderate assistance to avoid blurring the responsiveness of the pedal. The rack and pinion steering gives an outstandingly compact turning circle and answers instantly to small movements of the wheel.

The engine is a very sturdy seven-bearing six-cylinder with a single chain-driven overhead camshaft. For balance, evenly-spaced firing impulses, and a pure exhaust note, the straight-six has no peer unless you can go to 12 cylinders. If it is mounted fairly well back, to obtain an advantageous weight distribution, it does require a rather long bonnet, which gives the Datsun an E-type look on a smaller scale. The gearbox is in unit with the engine and has the now generally accepted arrangement with fifth speed out on the right and forward.

Though the car is low, the large doors give quite easy entry and there is ample seat adjustment for the tallest driver. Similarly, the width at shoulder level is generous indeed. The controls are very well placed but the scuttle is on the high side which, coupled with the length of the bonnet, makes the driver feel that he is sitting rather low. Distance pieces are provided to bolt between the seat and its mountings, which would be almost essential for the smaller mortals and probably advantageous for others. The seats have the high backs which are not universally popular but are presumably intended for the US market. The interior is attractively trimmed and the instrument panel, with its impressive show of proper round dials, tells the enthusiast everything he wants to know.

Like most Japanese cars, the 240 Z has a very potent starter motor that brings instant results. The engine is outstandingly flexible, as a good six should be, allowing the car to wander along in traffic at 10 mph on the direct fourth gear. It gives a lot of power between 4000 and 6000 rpm, the curve starting to droop at 6500 rpm, but it remains smooth and unhurried anywhere within its range.

The Datsun reaches and holds 120 mph very easily and I covered some quite long distances at this speed. If everything is just right, an honest 125 or 126 mph can eventu-

ally be reached but the engine cannot over-rev on fifth gear. I normally selected that ratio at about 100 mph and there seems no point in retaining the direct drive up to its ultimate 120 mph, except to enjoy the *panache* of changing up after vanquishing a pugnacious opponent. On the *Autoroute du Nord*, I found nobody who could quite match my speed, but two Citroëns *à injection* and a V8 Mercedes caused me to travel for many kilometres with my foot hard on the floor, which the 240 Z seemed to enjoy as much as I did.

The ride is hard at low speeds but remarkably comfortable at high speeds on bad French roads. On some surfaces, such as the *autoroutes*, there is a complete absence of road noise, but on others, notably some British

motorways with a sandpaper non-skid finish, the sound level is high. The engine is quiet though the exhaust occasionally blares at high speeds on the overrun. In contrast, the gearbox whines on the indirects and there is an occasional clonk from the driveshafts. There is a notable absence of wind noise below 100 mph but at 120 mph it is quite prominent. To summarise, the Datsun is not as refined as an expensive luxury saloon but it is by no means noisy compared with other sports cars.

With quick, responsive steering and excellent independent rear suspension, the car is a delight to handle. The degree of understeer is very moderate and there is enough power to alter all that. In this connection, the 5-speed box always provides the right gear

Thanks to some notable rally successes the 240Z is already regarded as quite a formidable car.

SPO 137K

The seven-bearing six-cylinder engine is very flexible with a lot of power between 4000 and 6500 rpm.

ratio and the change is easy and certain. The car corners very fast with extremely little roll, the sensitive steering giving a wonderful feeling of control on wet roads. For ideal handling, the steering should be sufficiently light and high-geared to give a suspicion of kickback over the worst bumps, which is exactly how the Datsun is arranged; it is this steering which lifts it head and shoulders above its competitors. The brakes are powerful and fade-free, the independent suspension allowing them to be used to full advantage.

The heating is powerful and the fresh air vents are well arranged at the sides and centre of the instrument panel. The blower works both on the heated air and the cold breathing air, running sufficiently quietly to be inaudible at its lowest speed. It takes some juggling, however, to obtain warm feet, a demisted screen, and cool air to breathe, all at one time. The quartz-halogen lamps are very effective and when they were dipped nobody flashed at me in France, though I had naughtily forgotten to change them over. The engine is completely untemperamental and idled happily to itself in the worst traffic blocks that Paris could impose.

Thanks to some notable rally successes, the 240 Z is already regarded as quite a formidable car. I have driven one of the works rally cars which, though certainly having rather more power, was remarkably standard in most respects. The appearance attracts attention and the spoilers, front and rear, are more than a styling gimmick if one can judge by the steadiness of the car at speed.

For sheer driving enjoyment, I place this sports car very high indeed. Though it is a thoroughly practical fast tourer, nothing has been done to blunt its sporting character, and therein lies its charm. To the fat tycoon, who drives as he works out his next big deal, the 240 Z has nothing to offer, but to the man who still regards driving as a pleasure and an art, it promises unending enjoyment.

SPECIFICATION AND PERFORMANCE DATA

Car tested : Datsun 240 Z 2-seater sports coupé; price £2,389.37, including tax.
Engine : Six cylinders, 83 mm x 73.7 mm (2393 cc); single chain-driven overhead camshaft; twin Hitachi constant-vacuum carburetters; compression ratio 9 to 1; 151 bhp (gross) at 5600 rpm.
Transmission : Single dry plate clutch; 5-speed all-synchromesh gearbox, ratios 0.85, 1.0, 1.31, 1.86 and 2.96 to 1; hypoid final drive, ratio 3.90 to 1.
Chassis : Combined steel body and chassis; independent suspension of all four wheels by MacPherson struts, lower wishbones, and coil springs with telescopic dampers; rack and pinion steering; Girling disc front and drum rear brakes with vacuum Servo; bolt-on disc wheels fitted 175-14 radial ply tyres.
Equipment : 12-volt lighting and starting; speedometer; rev-counter; clock; ammeter; oil pressure, water temperature and fuel gauges; heating, demisting and ventilation system with electrically-heated rear window; 2-speed windscreen wipers and washers; flashing direction indicators with hazard warning; reversing lights.
Dimensions : Wheelbase, 7 ft 6½ in; track, 4 ft 5¾ in; overall length, 13 ft 7 in; width, 5 ft 4 in; weight, 1 ton.
Performance : Maximum speed, 125 mph; speeds in gears, fourth 120 mph, third 90 mph, second 65 mph, first 40 mph; standing quarter-mile, 15.8 s; acceleration, 0-30 mph 2.9 s, 0-50 mph 5.9 s, 0-60 mph 8.0 s, 0-80 mph 14.5 s, 0-100 mph 24.0 s.
Fuel consumption : 18 to 26 mpg.

The interior is impressive and the array of well appointed dials tells the enthusiast everything he wants to know.

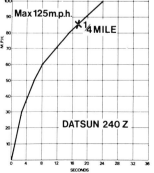

MOTOR week ending July 29, 1978

OLD SAMURIS

. . . never die nor fade away; they just get faster. Jeremy Sinek has been on the road in a car that's in its prime — at over 100,000 miles

WE'RE A SPOILT LOT us *Motor* noters. Seldom do we drive a test car that is anything but in the prime of its life, and rarely do we have a live with a car 'til the point where its joints begin to creak, its springs to sag, and the energy ebbs from its engine. And having once parted with a car, we don't usually expect ever to sit behind its wheel again.

But in the case of ol' FFA, we jumped at the chance. We first tested the old fellow (I know, a car is usually a "she", but there is nothing even remotely feminine about FFA) in August 1973. Property of one Spike Anderson, the car had been purchased new in April '73 as a latter-day Healey substitute by Spike, who ran it in for 1,000 miles and then turned it into a Super Samuri.

We tested it, with the result that the usually loquacious McCarthy found himself stumbling for words to describe the performance, eventually settling for "Amazing, astonishing . . . Definitely mind-blowing." Small wonder, for by dint of a gas-flowed (but standard-valved) head, three 40 DCOE Webers and a six-branch exhaust, Spike had transformed an already quick car into a snarling monster that sprinted from zero to 60 mph in 6.4 sec, and to 100 mph in 17.0 sec. Additionally, the suspension had been tweaked, a front air dam welded on, and the exterior treated

to a simple, yet highly effective custom paint job — all part of the Super Samuri package.

At that time the brakes were standard, and we soon found they were simply no match for the car's new-found 190 bhp performance. Spike soon put a stop to that: Lockheed Formula 1 ventilated front discs and four-pot calipers are now an integral part of the full house Samuri package, (of which Spike has now sold the best part of 60 examples.)

Five years on, FFA is still a Super Samuri, only more so. It is also 8,000 miles the wrong side of 100,000 old. Those years and miles have been hard and incident full, and the car's history is worth retelling.

In that first year or so, when FFA wasn't being used as Spike's daily transport, it was being road tested by motoring magazines, or at weekends competed in various forms of motor sport, mainly mod-sports. However, like many tuners, Spike found himself floundering financially in the wake of the fuel crisis, and in late 1974 he had to sell the car. It went to a suitably appreciative new owner, who continued to sprint, hill-climb and race it, helping take the tally of mod-sports races to 39, of which the car only ever failed to finish one (when the brake fluid boiled).

A year or two later Spike purchased another Datsun, LAL 909K,

in a sorry condition. For one thing, the engine had no oil pressure — mainly because there wasn't any oil in the sump: after flushing out the engine and putting in new oil, a healthy pressure was restored. On strip down, no wear was found on the 62,000 mile engine, so Spike just

fitted new rings and shells, honed the bores, and rebuilt the engine in 190 bhp Super Samuri form. And went motor racing. The car finished 20th overall in the 6-hour International at Silverstone, and the next day Spike went shopping in it.

continued over

MOTOR week ending July 29, 1978

But over the next year Spike and Co decided to go the whole hog and turn the car into a proper racer, albeit on the lowest possible budget. Suspension was treated to still lower and stiffer springs (DTV Rally springs for the Magnum!), solid bushes for the strut upper mountings, and home-brewed uprated dampers. For £150 they had a full-race suspension. For the engine they selected, from David Newman's range, the wildest cam they dared use and still keep a standard bottom end (7,000 rpm limit). In conjunction with this road/rally cam, Spike changed the 40 DCOE Webers for a set of 45 DHLA Dellortos and fitted an unsilenced exhaust. On borrowed wheels and racing rubber the car produced 163 bhp at the rear wheels (about 215 at the flywheel), and again went motor racing — in the 1977 6-hour International at Brands Hatch. At one point LAL 909K was lying 6th overall, but its race was ended prematurely when it crashed on a patch of oil and was written off.

But it takes more than that to keep an old Z-car down, for in the meantime FFA had come home. The third owner had trailered the car to Spike's place, the car suffering from a severe case of no go. For Spike it was the return of an old and dearly loved friend, and the car never left his yard: the chap hadn't wanted to sell it, but must have been moved by the tears in Spike's eyes . . .

By now ol' FFA's engine was tired, so Spike took the engine and suspension from the broken racer and dropped it all into FFA. To Spike's surprise, as much as anyone's, the car turned out to be quite driveable on the road. On Dellorto's suggestion, the 45s were changed for 48s, giving an extra 8 bhp and even more torque, and in that form, with 8-inch wheels, 225/60 HR 14 tyres, full roll cage, fire extinguisher, 78,000 miles on the engine, and 108,000 miles on the rest of the car, we renewed our acquaintance with the old brute.

Nobody could pretend that FFA isn't showing *some* signs of age: rattles and creaks abound, there is backlash in the transmission, and disc run-out makes the brakes distinctly juddery at "normal" speeds.

But given the space to unsheath the cutting edge of its power, this old soldier will still leave for dead almost anything the Supercar makers can put up against it — or go down fighting. After all, it is still only a 2.4-litre engine, and Sam is heavier now than

Above: although the interior is equipped with all the necessary racing goodies — full roll cage, fire extinguishers, bucket seat and full harness — Super Sam retains the original trim and facia. **Below:** chubby tyres give tenacious roadholding but call for strong-arm tactics around town.

in '73. Older, too, and those wide wheels and tyres have sapped some of the extra power. Yet even so, and in spite of a malfunctioning tachometer and top end misfire, we shaved vital tenths of seconds off Sam's '73 times to record 0-60 mph in 6.2 sec and 0-100 mph in 15.8, with the kilometre post reached just 26.7 sec from rest, the speed approaching 120 mph and still rising very swiftly.

You do need space to use this performance, however, for the power is very much concentrated in the upper half of the rev range. Above 3500 rpm the engine screams exultantly and the revs rocket to the red line. Below 2500 rpm the engine is astonishingly tractable: it won't take kindly to full throttle, but by feeding it in progressively we achieved respectable 4th gear figures like 20-40 mph in 8.0 sec and 30-50

mph in 7.6: it'll pull from 1000 rpm, and ticks over steadily and reliably at just 700 rpm. Only in the 2500-3500 rpm range is there a problem, caused by a rough patch in the carburation that is amply illustrated by the fourth gear figures between 50 and 70 mph. On a fast open road you can get round it, but in the clutter of town traffic it can be an embarrassment.

Handling, too, is best suited to swooping through long, sweeping open road bends, where the car sits four-square on the road, the SP Supers stick like glue and a caress of the wheel is sufficient to steer it round the bend. On roundabouts and street corners the race suspension geometry and huge tyres make the steering very heavy, and it kicks back and understeers, though oversteer can always be induced under power and the tight limited slip diff causes marked power on/ power off changes of attitude.

But the race suspension does not make for an intolerable ride: very firm, certainly, but harshness is filtered out and the jolts delivered to the driver in palatable form. It is better at high speed than low, as are the brakes. Pedal weight, feel and progression are well nigh perfect: braking from 130 mph at the end of the MIRA straights was achieved with blissful confidence, but at sublegal speeds the brakes were rough and juddery, though still effective. A quick skim of the discs would work wonders.

Methinks we still haven't seen the last of FFA. When last spoken to, Spike was muttering about changing up to 2.8-litres, using a short engine from the 280C saloon. Suitably breathed upon, 250 bhp should be on the cards. In the meantime, he continues to endow customers' Zs with 190 and 223 bhp Super Samuri conversions in his Olde Worlde garage in the Northamptonshire village of Croughton: you'll find him there at the place called Park End, or on the other end of Croughton 403.

And if you happen to be passing that way in your shiny new Supercar, and come across the meanest looking Datsun you ever saw in your life, think twice before taking it on: put age before beauty, and avoid egg on your face.

Know what I mean?

PERFORMANCE

	Sam '78	Sam '74	240Z
Max. speed mph	150*	140*	125.1
Acceleration			
mph	sec	sec	sec
0-30	2.5	2.4	2.8
0-40	3.3	3.6	4.4
0-50	4.7	4.9	6.3
0-60	6.2	6.4	8.3
0-70	8.1	8.5	11.3
0-80	10.2	10.7	14.3
0-90	12.6	13.4	19.1
0-100	15.8	17.0	23.9
0-110	20.2	—	—
0-120	27.1	—	—
Standing ¼ mile	14.6	14.8	16.2
Standing km.	26.7	27.3	29.9
In fourth			
20-40	8.0	—	6.9
30-50	7.6	—	6.9
40-60	11.2	5.7	7.2
50-70	14.3	6.5	7.4
60-80	11.1	6.9	7.6
70-90	7.0	6.1	8.1
80-100	7.0	7.0	10.0
90-110	8.5	—	—
Overall mpg	14.0	20.4	25.7
*Estimate			

Super Profile

Road test
by John Bolster

Datsun 260Z body pressings remain unaltered though the interior is re-styled.

Smoother quicker 260Z

It is well known that, during the past four years, the Datsun 240Z has become the world's most popular sports car, largely through having won almost a monopoly of the lucrative USA market. Britain now has no car to equal it, except perhaps the TVR, which is made in rather limited quantities. The Japanese car hit the jackpot because it had a lot of performance yet a moderate fuel consumption, it was small and of very sporting appearance, but was completely practical for town use or business journeys.

In replacing the 240Z by the 260Z, the manufacturers have been careful to make as few changes as possible. It was necessary to

make some basic alterations, in the interest of reducing pollution, and the compression ratio had to be lowered to suit lead-free fuel. To reduce the performance would not be acceptable so the engine size was increased by fitting a longer-throw crank, the stroke going up by 5.3 mm. The new engine meets all the requirements and there is a small increase both in maximum power and torque, which has permitted a change in final drive ratio from 3.9 to 3.7 to 1. The two lowest gears of the five-speed box have also been closed up a little and a tyre size that puts more rubber on the road has been adopted.

The same body pressings have been re-

tained, though the interior has been re-styled in accordance with the latest trends. As always, the suspension is independent all round on the MacPherson system and the rack and pinion steering needs less than three turns from lock to lock. There is an anti-roll bar in front and the springs have been slightly stiffened, partly because of a small increase in weight. The straight-six engine cannot be mounted too far forward or the weight distribution would be impaired, so the fairly long bonnet must be accepted, but this is a traditional sports car feature which many people still admire. The scuttle is fairly high and a short driver might want to raise the seat.

The body is strictly a two-seater, with enough room for the biggest occupants. The opening rear window is controlled by telescopic struts and there are straps to secure the luggage on a spacious platform which is, however, in view of miscreants outside. The spare wheel is enclosed in a case beneath this platform, alongside the petrol tank. Everything is well arranged for the driver's convenience and a comfortable position can be found by people of varying sizes.

The choke must be used for a while until the engine is warm, but the unit then shows true six-cylinder flexibility. For city driving, a change of leverage might be beneficial in the throttle linkage, the butterflies tending to open rather sharply from the closed position unless a little care is exercised. The five-speed gearbox is superb, with a light change and close ratios. Fourth and fifth gears can be used at quite low speeds, which is perhaps why the bigger engine actually seems to be more economical than its predecessor.

One might expect the already good acceleration to be improved and certainly the car pulls its high gearing well. Yet, the combination of this ratio with the wider tyres makes a racing start difficult, unless one is willing to punish the clutch. This I refuse to do, and so there was a slight tendency to fluff just after the getaway; below 60 mph I was therefore not quite able to equal my figures for the 240Z. However, life isn't all racing starts and a 40 mph bottom gear is ideal for sharp bends.

The engine peaks at 5600 rpm and there seems little point in going over 6000 rpm, even when obtaining the best possible acceleration figures. Curiously enough, the rev-counter is marked yellow from 6500 to 7000, where the red starts, but this seems somewhat unwise with the longer stroke now adopted. I went up to 7000 rpm once, but never again, for the crank goes through a torsional period at around that speed. It is possible that the rev-counter of the test car was reading slow at the top end, and that I over-revved in consequence, but I would prefer the red section to start 500 rpm earlier. The gear speeds in my data panel are given for 6500 rpm in the lower gears but the car will not exceed 5700 rpm in fifth, so the new gear ratio is just about spot on. The highly satisfactory 127 mph maximum of the 260Z is just 2 mph up on the 240Z.

The Datsun is perhaps a bit noisy when accelerating, though the exhaust note is a joy to the enthusiast and it does not seem to attract unwelcome attention. Cruising on a high gear, the car is delightfully effortless, and at 90 mph on a whiff of throttle it is outstandingly quiet for a sports car. On bumpy roads some thumping is heard and sandpaper surfaces create a roaring noise, but wind noise is only audible above about 100 mph. The machine is very steady at speed but side winds tend to deflect it when travelling at over 110 mph. Such speeds are somewhat academic at the moment, unfortunately.

The 260Z corners very well, perhaps with a shade less understeer than its predecessor. The steering is quite light, except when taking very sharp corners; sensitive and quick, it is responsible for much of the car's character. A tail-out attitude can be achieved on really fast bends, but the rear-

The 260Z corners well with less understeer than its predecessor.

Road test

end sticks down well with no tendency to break away, though a succession of bumps may call for a little correction. The ride is fairly firm at low speeds but smooths out at higher cruising rates, though the 260Z always feels like a sports car.

The brakes are entirely adequate for normal road use and are always smooth and silent in action. Racing is another matter and a determined driver might well make them fade under such conditions. This is, after all, a pretty fast car and no light weight, so the brakes have a job of work to do. For driving at ten-tenths on a circuit, a very expensive installation with ventilated discs would be justified. This is a road test, however, and I don't think that the average owner will get anywhere near the fading point — there's plenty of warning if it does begin to happen, anyway.

Similarly, the lights are reasonable for fairly fast motoring but better ones are available for the enthusiast who wants to gild the lily. In standard form, this Datsun is a fast car that will delight the man who enjoys a really potent sports model for his everyday driving. It would be much heavier if it were deprived of its roof, so a fixed-head coupe seems to be the only solution if maximum performance is required.

It must be admitted that I needed two Datsuns for this road test and the one in the photographs is not the one that gave the performance figures. The first car just didn't like me — it made me walk home in the dark when its lights failed and it sulked when I pressed the stopwatches for speed tests. During all our own troubles, it's nice to know that the Japanese can make Friday cars, too, but the second one was as fast and reliable as we have come to expect of Datsuns.

SPECIFICATION AND PERFORMANCE DATA

Car tested : Datsun 260Z two-seater coupe, price £2,895 including car tax and V.A.T.
Engine : Six cylinders, 83 mm x 79 mm (2565 cc) ; compression ratio, 8.3 to 1 ; 162 bhp (gross) at 5600 rpm ; single chain-driven overhead camshaft ; two Hitachi horizontal SU-type carburetters.
Transmission : Single dry plate clutch ; five-speed all synchromesh gearbox with central change, ratios 0.86, 1.0, 1.31, 1.90, 2.91, and 3.38 to 1 ; hypoid final drive, ratio 3.70 to 1.
Chassis : Combined steel body and chassis ; independent suspension of all wheels by MacPherson struts incorporating telescopic dampers and coil springs, with lower wishbones ; anti-roll bar in front ; rack and pinion steering ; servo-assisted disc front and drum rear brakes ; bolt-on steel disc wheels, fitted 195/70 VR 14 tyres.
Equipment : Speedometer ; rev-counter, water temperature, oil pressure, and fuel gauges ; ammeter ; clock ; heating, demisting, and ventilation system with heated rear window ; intermittent and two-speed windscreen wipers and washers ; flashing direction indicators ; reversing lights.
Dimensions : Wheelbase, 7 ft 6.7 in ; track (front) 4 ft 5.3 in, (rear) 4 ft 5 in ; overall length, 13 ft 6.8 in ; width, 5 ft 4.2 in ; weight, 2,425 lb.
Performance : Maximum speed, 127 mph. Speeds in gears Fourth, 125 mph ; third, 96 mph ; second, 65 mph ; first, 43 mph. Standing quarter-mile, 15.7 s. Acceleration 0-30 mph, 3.8 s ; 0-50 mph, 6.2 s ; 0-60 mph, 8.2 s ; 0-80 mph, 14.4 s ; 0-100 mph, 23.8 s.
Fuel consumption : 20 to 28 mpg.

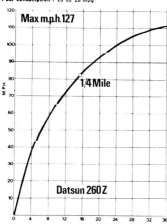

Datsun 260Z — Max m.p.h. 127 — 1/4 Mile (graph: MPH vs SECONDS)

Above : High scuttle for short drivers. Below : Traditional long bonnet appearance.

2565 cc straight six engine produces 162 bhp at 5600 rpm.

OWNER'S VIEW

So what is it about owning a Z which makes so many owners into fanatics? There is only one way to find out and that is to ask, so I contacted a number of owners to get the facts straight from the horse's mouth.

On asking 'Why were you first interested in the Z?' the replies took two directions. Initial interest seems to have been based upon striking styling, and then rapidly followed by surprise at the price. Lynne Godber, the British Z Club's Chairman, and owner of a concours '71 240Z, admits to being 'instantly arrested' when she saw her first 240. 'I had never seen a Z before, so when I walked round the front I was not prepared for that long bulging bonnet and headlamp cowls. It immediately struck me as a baby E-Type and, on closer questioning of an expert, I found it was in the category of affordable.' Peter Leer, who runs a late '77 260Z 2 + 2 in 'semi-regular everyday use' was first interested, 'because it is a great-looking individual sportscar ... and is above all affordable'. While Kevin Bristow, who has owned two 240s, one a very late model in first class order which he is still running, puts it very succinctly: 'The 240Z is a one-off design and offers tremendous value for money'.

When owners were asked where they bought their cars, answers varied enormously, from Peter Leer's 'from an ex-girlfriend in 1982' to John Toms' reply that his 240Z was, 'the very last 1971 model Z imported to the UK (Chassis No. HS30 01363),' when he bought it new. Some buyers were lucky; Ian Pearce decided to go motor racing, and chose the 'Post Historic Roadsports Championship' for vehicles manufactured prior to 1971. He purchased the car from an *Exchange & Mart* advertisement in 1982 without realizing that his 1970 model was one of only two eligible!

The next question involved the car's condition when purchased and what had to be done to put it right. Graham Miller bought his 260Z in 1984 and describes its condition as 'abandoned'. It required, 'a new clutch, exhaust, brake pipes all round, selector on second gear, battery, starter motor overhaul, blown head gasket replaced, new headlamp bowls, plus many smaller bits and pieces. The car was finally resprayed, old paint being removed right down to bare metal'. When asked if it would have been better to buy an example in better condition, he replied, 'In my case – no; the bonus of the registration '260Z', being the deciding factor'.

In fact most owners who have undertaken major restoration work admit it would have been wiser to buy a car in better condition, but all had good reasons for not doing so. Ian Pearce's Historic Racer required 'a new chassis underpan due to rust. I couldn't buy these items so we made up a new chassis, and when offering it up to the body we were only $1/8$ inch out of line.'

On the other hand, some owners go out of their way to make work for themselves. I asked Mike Feeney what had made him build his very special 240Z. Mike had previously owned TRs – a TR2, TR4 and TR6 – which 'gave

way to a succession of American cars, but lingering memories of a 240Z in a Swansea dealer's showroom brought me to the combination of the Z with the most popular American V8, the Chevrolet small block. Totally logical really.' So a very arduous project got under way. Says Mike, 'Performance from the V8 is obviously impressive; we have just run our best time at Santa Pod this weekend, which was 13.97 seconds at 100.2mph. 0 – 60mph by prediction is probably around 6 seconds, maybe less. Top speed with direct drive through the auto box, a 3.75:1 Jaguar diff and the 6000rpm rev limit is only about 120mph, but it gets there quick!' When I asked Mike what he would do differently were he doing the job again, he replied, 'I wouldn't use fibreglass front wings, I would advise steel for the best finish, as rippling is apparent after painting and exposure to heat and sun'. I asked, 'Do you have any problem getting parts?', and immediately wished I hadn't. 'I don't think the Z Club's spare parts collator should admit to having problems obtaining parts!' said Mike. So I put the question to Luke Borg, who also has a 5.7 litre V8 240Z as well as one of the few 280Zs in Britain, 'It's much easier and cheaper to buy body parts now than, say, three years ago because there are now metal wings, door skins, etc. which are not Datsun made and are half the price. It is very much cheaper to rebuild a Z body today than it was a few years ago.' Asked about his V8 conversion, Luke said, 'It's a very expensive, but very enjoyable toy. It has the performance of a 911 Turbo, but £25,000 cheaper!' Generally it was agreed that spares have not proved a problem due to availability, only due to price.

It has often been said that the Z is very reliable so, to answer this point, I turned to John Toms; at the time of writing John has covered over 155,000 miles in his '71 240Z. John says, 'The engine is totally original, barring the replacement head gasket at 29,000, and it still burns no oil. The gearbox and back axle have never been touched. I have had a reconditioned radiator and two clutches – one at 86,000 and the other at 152,000. Brake wear has been incredibly good. The first set lasted me for 46,000 miles, the second to 86,000 and the third to 140,000. I had new shock absorbers at 86,000 but, in retrospect, I wish I had Koni shocks fitted instead of the standard Datsun ones. As to what I find appealing about the car; in order I would select the following: styling, practicability, driveability and handling, performance and, finally, reliability. The last I have found to be incredible. Cost of ownership? Very reasonable.'

Lynne Godber's car has, like John's, been well cared for and maintained, both mechanically and bodily, as required. During recent years Lynne's car, affectionately known as 'Zep', has had the rear wheel arches replaced along with the driver's door skin, but further problems followed, 'due to my misjudgement of my new, smaller garage. I wrote off the near-side front wing and door skin. Replacing these panels led to the discovery that the chassis leg had rusted out near the bulkhead. Inspection of the other side proved a similar welding job was needed. Also, the floor pan on the driver's side. This welding proved to be the first major renovation the Z needed after 13 years on the road!' Lynne's successes in concours events must be a good advertisement as the bodywork is looked after by her husband, who is a partner in a body repair business.

Ian Fuller is close to finishing a total restoration of his 260Z, and seems to have similar experiences to others to recount, 'All the mechanicals were excellent, but the usual rust problems were evident.' Asked about the Z Club, Ian replied positively, 'It's very useful to be a member; there's the discount of 10 or 15 per cent on parts, etc., also the meetings enable Z enthusiasts to get together to discuss problems and show off their cars.'

On the practicality side, the Z must score better than almost any sportscar due to a high level of standard equipment and good luggage space but, like most classics, the Z is in many cases a second car – a hobby – so practicality is a small consideration. Says Clive Standish, owner of a very highly modified 240Z boasting a big-valve, high compression, gas-flowed cylinder head, high lift camshaft, triple Dellorto 45 mm carbs, six branch exhaust and competition suspension, 'I use the car only at weekends (with a few exceptions), on trips to Z Club meetings, evenings out at country pubs and the like, preferably where I can give her a good run! For what I want, it serves its purpose; that is sheer exhilarating driving. Mind you, it isn't always practical – for instance I'm hesitant about parking it in an unknown area for fear of theft or vandalism. The obvious point is that, being a two-seater, it does restrict, but one can work that to one's advantage!'

On the performance and handling side, John Toms had this to say: 'The greatest joy I have found with my car, in all my 155,000 miles, is the pure pleasure of actually driving it. The handling and driveability have always been to a high standard'. Said Lynne, 'In one word, excellent. The Z feels a heavy, secure car and passes this feeling on to the driver. I have the confidence to put the Z into a tight corner and know that the back end will stick to the road.' In fact

'confidence' was a word used by more than a few owners, and 'strong acceleration' was given a plus point by several.

Did our owners have any advice for potential owners? Plenty:-

Kevin Bristow – 'Consider it carefully, it's a responsibility, needing constant attention, money and effort.'

Mike Feeney – 'Buy the best you can afford. Check every possible rust trap carefully – at least twice. Don't trust dealers. Try to buy from an enthusiast. Join the Club.'

John Toms – 'Change the engine oil and filter every 3,000 miles without fail. Extravagant some say, but it appears to have rewarded me.'

Peter Leer – 'Don't modify the car unless you are getting significant returns and can afford to do a proper job. Don't underestimate the performance.' Luke Borg – 'If you are going to keep the car a very long time then spend a fair amount to buy one, then spend some more on the engine, body and handling and, at the end of the day, you have an immaculate, very fast and good-looking sportscar which will outperform cars costing much, much more.'

Lynne Godber – 'Buy one!'

BUYING

So you want to buy a Datsun Z. What should you consider? Firstly, which model should you go for? This must depend upon what use you intend to put the vehicle to. For a general duty, everyday car go for a late model, bearing in mind that you can select either a two-seater or a 2+2. On later cars the trim is sturdier, the ride softer and the level of interior refinement higher. On the other hand, if the car is to be a second car or a weekend toy in which simply to enjoy the pleasures of open road motoring, find a good early example. In general, the earlier the better; in the UK certainly pre-May 1972, after which the requirements of US emission control started to have their effect on all markets' models. But remember, a concours 240Z is a responsibility, not just enjoyable transport!

Finding a good early 240Z is not easy. They were produced long before factory rustproofing was commonplace and, as a result, they have not fared too well from a corrosion point of view. This, added to the inexplicable fact that, in the UK anyway, the cars were generally not very well cared for, has resulted in the numbers diminishing substantially.

Body

Being of a unitary construction, major repairs are very expensive to carry out. Major panels, such as the rear wings, forming part of the welded structure including both the tailgate and doorway frames, are frighteningly expensive. The rear wheel arches of the 240Z, particularly in areas of bad weather, had a tendency to rust badly. The cause was a design/construction fault which resulted in pockets forming between the spot welds on the inner arch to wing seam. These pockets inevitably filled with mud, salt and water providing ideal conditions for rust. As the problem was inside the seam it was invisible until tell-tale rust bubbles started to form on the outside of the wheel arch. By this time it was too late, the damage was done. As a result, most 240Zs have had rear arch repairs and this area should be carefully examined to establish how well the repairs were carried out. This problem was overcome on the 260Z and 280Z as a different construction method was employed which eliminated the offending pockets. Steel repair panels are now available for this area and fit very well. When fitting it is advisable to seam-weld the panels to seal the joint and prevent recurrence.

Working forward from here we come to the sills. Although relatively inexpensive in themselves, the fitting is expensive as the sill extends under both front and rear wings which hence require partial removal. If fitting rear wheel arch repair panels, it is advisable to consider the condition of the sills as the area of the rear wing which has to be cut away is the same section which lies over the sill.

Structural areas ahead of the windscreen where careful examination is necessary are the main longitudinal box sections which run from under the floor and extend forward from the bulkhead at the bottom of the inner wings. These rails, combined with the inner wings and upper flitch panels, provide the bulk of the strength in the front of the vehicle and effectively provide the support, via a crossmember, to the engine, suspension and steering gear. Their condition is therefore paramount to the survival of the vehicle unless a hugely expensive repair is undertaken. The section in the vicinity of the front anti-roll bar mounts seems to give the most trouble but, if the corrosion is confined, a reasonable repair can usually be made.

The inner wings themselves can also give problems as they join the main rails at 90 degrees and, in fact, form one side of each rail's square section. If extensive corrosion has taken place in the rails the inner wings will probably also be similarly affected. The flitch, which is also a box section, and which runs along the other side of the inner wing at the top, can also give problems. This can be checked by reaching through the wheel arches. As these panels are out of sight a good cosmetic repair is not essential, and therefore less expensive to carry out.

Many vehicles with strut front suspension suffer corrosion on the top of the turrets. This is a problem the Zs have not suffered. However, the turrets do rust lower down, in the bottom 4-5 inches. This can be patched at reasonable expense but, once again, the inner wing will corrode due to moisture being trapped between the two panels.

The floorpan itself gives few problems, but the footwells and underfloor box sections are well worth checking.

The next parts of the bodywork to consider are the bolt-on rather than welded panels. These are obviously easier and therefore cheaper to deal with. Let's start at the back again with the tailgate. The only area of concern is the seam where the frame and the outer skin are folded together on the rear edge. Rust can often be found here, probably as a result of poor paint coverage.

The doors can suffer the same fault as the tailgate, but along the bottom edge, and if in poor condition can be repaired by the letting-in of a repair panel which replaces the bottom 6 inches of the outer skin.

Of the bolt-on panels, the front wings are the major concern. Areas to watch are the 'sill' area behind the wheel arch, the area round the repeater indicator, the joints around the headlight pods and front quarter valances, the flat top area above the wheel arch and a vertical line midway between the wheel arch and the door. Problems in these areas are again caused, like the rear arches, by mud traps. Many cars have had very much cheaper fibreglass wings fitted; if so, deduct much money!

Bonnets usually stand up well with the exception of the rather vulnerable leading edge which can rust from inside as well as be subject to parking knocks and stone chips.

Mechanical

On the mechanical side the Z series has proved very much more durable. The engine itself is remarkably sturdy and, because of its simple design, is easy for the home mechanic to attend to. The main components of the bottom end are pretty near trouble-free. One hundred thousand mile engines have been rebuilt requiring only new piston rings, bearings and oil seals; the crank, rods, pistons and bores being in good order. The cylinder head generally requires decoking and rebuilding at the 70-80,000 mile mark, at which age the camshaft and valve stem oil seals often need replacement. Cam wear is largely the result of the engine oil being changed too infrequently. Sludge in the oil

builds up and the flow through the spray bar is impeded, resulting in the cam running with insufficient lubricant. Later cars will fare better in this respect as the oil flow system was altered so that the oil flowed through larger holes in the camshaft lobes and ensured that a healthy flow was maintained. Early cars which have had the camshaft replaced will probably have the cam with the better oil flow, and this set-up plus the spray bar probably provides the best all-round lubrication.

Early spray bars had a tendency for part of the tube to come loose, resulting in a leak and hence reduced oil flow where it was most needed. Care must be exercised when cylinder head maintenance is carried out to ensure the camshaft sprocket is correctly set up, otherwise inaccurate valve timing will result in reduced performance. When rebuilding the head at high mileage it would be worth replacing the timing chain and tensioners as these stretch and wear, making accurate valve timing difficult or impossible. Listen for a rattly chain when examining a potential purchase.

On the ancillary side, the starter motors seem indestructible, alternators normally give no trouble, but waterpumps suffer from worn shafts. If it's worn, you'll hear it! The viscous fan coupling can give problems; give it a turn to check that it is smooth running. The distributors are sturdy enough, as is the oil pump, with the exception of the internal spring which weakens in time. Replacement is a five minute job once the sump has been drained for a routine oil change, and may restore flagging oil pressure.

With regard to gearboxes, the earlier ones were more pleasant to use, but suffered one serious failing. The mainshaft gears are secured by a pair of locknuts torqued to 200 lb ft, and these have been known to work loose. The first sign is the loss of a gear,

followed by loud noises and a large bill unless the vehicle is immediately taken out of service. These gearboxes are easily identified as they have straight gear levers, whereas the later, stronger boxes had 'bent' levers. Apart from this, all the boxes are generally hardwearing and trouble-free – obviously check the synchromesh, but don't expect any serious wear to be apparent.

On the suspension and final drive side, there are no real weaknesses. The rear shock absorbers are more likely to be weak than the front due to the car's tendency to 'sit down' under acceleration. If replacing the rubber suspension bushes use 240Z ones as they were made from a harder compound than later ones, and provide a tauter feel.

Interior

Early Z seats were very prone to splitting, so a good original driver's seat is rare. A second-hand passenger seat can be converted by changing the runners and side brackets/recline mechanism for those from the worn driver's seat. Later seats were much improved, and should stand up to general wear better. Recline mechanism covers are regularly missing.

Other trim damage is likely to be confined to the hard plastic interior panels in the luggage area, probably caused by unsecured baggage being thrown around. Steering wheels and gear knobs have often been changed, so check these for originality, and switches and knobs are often missing or broken, particularly the choke knobs.

Value

Prices will vary more according to condition than age, and good 240Zs tend to be more expensive than the others. First class 240Zs are starting to command high prices now, and can only increase in value as more and more poorly cared for examples fall by the wayside and demand increases as the car's appeal as a classic grows. Generally, prices in the UK have been low, but in the US the Z has depreciated less than its competitors.

In the UK they therefore represent exceptional value for money. What other model can offer such looks, performance, handling and character for such a small outlay?

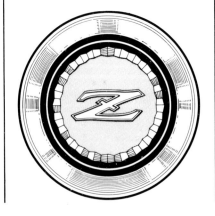

CLUBS, SPECIALISTS & BOOKS

Clubs

When seeking advice or information on any subject it is best to consult the expert, both professional and amateur. But where do you find the expert? Firstly, and probably most important, are the owners' clubs. These prosper in many countries, and the wealth of knowledge contained within the membership is quite astonishing. Ask almost any question of a keen member and, if he is unable to supply the answer, he will direct you to the member who does know. Whether it's a technical point, advice as to who can do a good paint job or where to obtain a spare part, the enthusiastic club member can provide the solution.

The Z Club – U.K.
Mark & Margaret Bukowski,
15 Curzon Road,
Ealing,
London.
Tel: 01-998-9616

Z Club – Australia,
Alan Steam,
Z-Car Workshop
Unit 2,
No. 2 Gunn Street,
Underwood,
Queensland 4119
Tel: 341-6100

Z Club – Germany
H.J. Malcherek
B-6231 Sulzbach,
Niederhofheimer,
VEG 5,
W. Germany

Z Club – Sweden
Thomas Alsterfalk,
Gasborn,
S-68096 Lesjofors

Z & ZX Club of America
P.O.Box 17617,
Greenville
S.C. 29606

Z CLub – New Zealand
Graham Collins,
Datsun Z Club Inc.,
P.O. Box 84030,
Logan Park,
Auckland 6

Z Club – USA
J.E. Casella
550 Lexington Avenue,
Clifton,
New Jersey, 070 11

Specialists

For the complex job that requires specialist knowledge, equipment and experience, such as engine building or performance tuning, consult the professional.

The best known UK specialists are Janspeed, Fourways Engineering, Mr. Z and Spike Anderson, the originator of the 'Super Samuri'. Fourways Engineering have specialised in Zs for many years and can, therefore, offer a very comprehensive service for all manner of performance tuning, suspension and brake conversions, and have full rolling road with microcomputer analysis available as well as full bodyshop facilities.

In the US the leading performance specialists include Bob Sharp Racing and Jim Cook Racing, while Wogco Carparts and Dobi offer a good range of accessories. Motorsport Auto hold a most comprehensive range of spares, including trim, badging, lamp lenses, body panels, accessories and a full selection of new and reconditioned mechanical components. Mr. Z keeps a similarly impressive list.

For turbo conversions there is, of course, Janspeed in the UK and Car Tech of Dallas, who offer a triple Mikuni carb conversion with turbo, intercooling and water injection. Scarab Automobiles of California specialize in V8 conversions, either by supplying a kit or building you a complete car.

Spike Anderson
Silverstone Circuit Ind. Est.
Silverstone,
Northants.
Tel: Silverstone 857178

Janspeed Engineering Ltd,
Castle Road,
Salisbury,
Wilts.
Tel: 0722 21833

Fourways Engineering Co.,
10-12 Maidstone Road,
Borough Green
Kent.
Tel: 0732 884288

Mr. Z,
35 Worthing Road,
Horsham,
W. Sussex.
Tel: 0403 56551/67774

Car Tech,
11144 Ables Lane,
Dallas,
Texas 75229
U.S.A.
Tel: (214) 620-0389

Dobi
320 Thor Place,
Brea,
California 92621,
U.S.A.
Tel: (714) 529-1977

Scarab Automobiles,
P.O. Box 9217
San Jose,
California 95157,
U.S.A.

Wogco Carparts,
2326 E. 44th St.,
Indianapolis,
IN 46205,
U.S.A.
Tel: (800) 428-1779

Jim Cook Racing,
5450 Katella Avenue
Bldg. 107,
Los Alamitos,
CA 90720, U.S.A.
Tel: (714) 828-9122

Motorsport Auto,
1139 West Collins Ave.,
Orange,
CA 92667,
U.S.A.
Tel: (714) 639-2620

**Bob Sharpe Parts &
Accessories Inc.,**
021 South Street,
Danbury,
CT 06810
U.S.A.
Tel: (203) 743-4487

Books

On the book front, there are a few that make interesting reading. Probably the most comprehensive is Ray Hutton's **The Z Series Datsuns,** now in its second edition, which includes the 280ZX and 300ZX models. Brooklands Books offer **Datsun 240Z and 260Z 1970-1977** and **Road and Track on Datsun Z**. Both provide a hundred or so pages of fact and opinion in the form of contemporary magazine article reprints. The American *Consumer Guide* series offers **Datsun Z Cars**, a 96 page hardback with numerous colour and monochrome photos.

For the home mechanic, workshop manuals are available from both Haynes and Autobooks. The Haynes version covers the various models in one book, whereas Autobooks provide separate publications for 240Z and 260Z. If tuning advice is something you seek, the most useful book is **Tuning Datsuns by Paul Davies.** Published by Speedsport, the book covers Datsuns in general, with sections on the L-Series engines and Z suspension, plus much useful general information on making a car go, handle and stop more effectively, and that's something we all want!

PHOTO GALLERY

1. Goertz's first car for Nissan, coded CSP311 but known as the Silvia, was, despite its very neat design, a failure. Launched in 1964, production was discontinued after just 550 had been made.

2. The Z's immediate predecessor, the Fairlady 2000 SR311, sold well in the States in the late sixties, boasting a 2-litre engine and 5-speed gearbox. A hardtop was optional.

1

2

3. Following Nissan's return to the original Goertz concept car, several full-size clay models were made. This one featured a rather heavy looking radiator opening, pop-up headlights, front wing louvres and was bumperless.

4. This prototype shows clearly the final Z shape even though it was short and rather high in the tail. Generally, it seems rather clumsy all over with huge wheel arches, wing louvres, angular rear quarter windows and 'slab' sides.

5. The Fairlady Z432. Note the Japanese specification wing mirrors, no spoilers and 'works' pattern alloy wheels which were available in some markets on ordinary Z models. The front towing eye, common to other Zs, is clearly visible.

6. Z432 from the rear quarter showing the distinctive twin exhausts unique to this model. Also visible are the ventilation outlets on the tailgate which were a feature of all pre-1971 Zs.

7. The Z's naturally low and mean looks enhanced by the camera's eye. This is the author's early 240Z.

8. Goertz designed the interior for large people. Here, Z Club member Peter Forder demonstrates the ease with which a tall driver can fit in. Peter is 6ft 7in!

9. The interior of a 1971 240Z. Note the choke lever position, with the earlier hand throttle blanked off next to it. During this era, the cigar lighter was positioned, with the ashtray, ahead of the gear lever. The steering wheel is non-standard.

10. The high-backed reclining bucket seats offered good support. The choke lever and silver topped ashtray are clearly visible on the centre console of the 240Z, dating it as after 1971.

11. The fuse box on a post-'71 240Z. Clipped to the right-hand side of the perspex cover is a fuse-changing tool. The driver's clutch foot rest is visible on the right.

7

8

9

10

11

12

13

12. The 240Z's 'wood-rim' and wooden gearknob. The non-reflective instruments are deeply recessed. This car has the Hitachi radio which was a UK option.

13. The Z's dash was well laid out from the driver's point of view as well as being aesthetically pleasing. This is an early 260Z 2+2 dash with 'leather wheel'.

14. Passenger door trim of a 240Z (right-hand drive) with armrest and grab handle. The recessed door opening lever falls very easily to hand. A grab handle is not fitted to the driver's door.

15. The 260Z featured revised trim for the doors along with many other areas. Here, a grab handle has been added and is now built into the armrest. Note also the second door opening handle positioned so it can be reached easily from the rear seats of this 2+2.

14

15

16. Nissan marketed the cars as either Nissan or Datsun, depending upon the country. Where the marque was Nissan, the bonnet badge simply stated 'Z'.

17. In Europe, Nissan branded the cars as Datsun and the bonnet badges echoed this fact.

18. Wing badge used on the Japanese 2-litre Fairlady Z. The 432 models had '432' added, centred above this badge.

19. The Datsun wing badge was employed on 240Z models only.

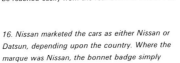

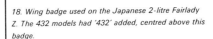

16

17

20. This 260Z badge replaced the Datsun badge on the front wings for the 260Z.

18

19

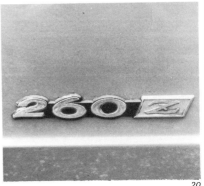

20

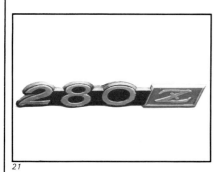

21

22

21. The US specification 280Z used this badge on the front wings. All the wing badges were plastic.

22. This very late 240Z has some components which are 260Z and original, as it was made during the changeover of production. Z club member, Kevin Bristow, owns this lovely example.

23. Datsun used several different wheels over the years. This is the pre-1972 240Z hubcap.

24. This hubcap was used for 240Zs from 1972 and for the 260Z and early 280Z models.

25. This alloy wheel was fitted as standard to all but the earliest 260Zs.

26. The fuel cap is found behind a hinged flap. A nice touch is the cap attached by a short chain and the rubber flap which folds down to protect the paintwork.

27. Most Zs had locking fuel flaps, but this unusual one is quite original and an example of one of the many inexplicable specification variations on early 240Zs.

23

28. Rear lamp cluster of the 240Z. Also visible is one of the pair of rear towing hooks. Some markets had over-riders fitted; the holes were blanked off with rubber grommets for those markets where vehicles were supplied without.

24

25

26

27

28

29

30

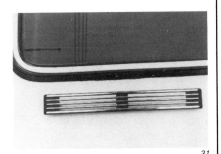

31

32

35

33

34

36

37

29. For the 260Z and 280Z, Datsun redesigned the rear lights and panel, splitting the reversing lights away from the main cluster. The rear panels on the 240Z were metal pressings whereas the later models featured moulded plastic panels.

30. Rear luggage compartment featuring strong nylon straps with which to secure luggage. Quilted vinyl covering of the rear turrets was also used on the transmission tunnel. 260Zs had plain grained vinyl.

31 & 32. The ventilation system of pre-1971 cars exits on each side of the tailgate via these slatted vents. The rear pillar badges on these cars were 240Z.

33. Once the slatted vents were discontinued, the ventilation outlets were built into the rear pillar badges. These were used on all two-seaters including the Japanese Fairlady Z which used these badges even when slatted vents were employed; being of 2 litres it could not use the 240Z badge.

34. All 2 + 2s used this badge for ventilation outlet covers.

35. The home market cars, as the American ones, had no spoilers. The number plate is illuminated from above, the bumper being plain. The vertical heated rear window elements clearly distinguish this as a vehicle of pre-1972 manufacture.

36. This rear view shows clearly the UK specification number plate lamps mounted on the bumper. The box above the plate is a dummy.

37. Models for most markets had the indicators built into the body under the front bumpers. European cars had these add-on ones instead.

38. Markets other than Europe had combined side lights/indicators under the front bumpers which, on this vehicle, has been removed and shows the joints in the panels.

39. The 280Zs and late US 260Zs had these huge 'federal' bumpers. Rather ungainly. Compare the length of the 280Z with the UK 260Z 2 + 2 for a shock!

40. Again, the 280Z. Rear wing indicator repeaters were standard on US cars which all came without front or rear spoilers.

38

39

40

41

41. The 280Z had much smoother front lower quarter panels due to the indicators being positioned in the radiator opening. These wheels are not standard.

42. Japanese market cars, for some unknown reason, had these rubber blocks fitted on the leading edge of the rear bumpers.

43 & 44. Rear spoiler badges of the 240Z. Note that Datsun is mounted on a raised area. The 260Z badge was in an identical style. Early Datsun badges were metal; later ones were plastic.

45. The rear quarter windows of the two-seaters do not open. The frames are stainless steel, as are those for the door windows, front and rear screen insets and wiper arms.

46. The opening quarter windows of the 2 + 2 are a very different shape to those of the two-seaters. They also have stainless steel surrounds.

47. This rear view clearly shows the well sculptured outline of the 240Z roof and the rear wing. Note the exceptional ground clearance for a car which looks so low, an advantage in rough rallying.

48. These bonnet vents, which were added for the 280Z, probably would have been advantageous on the earlier cars where high underbonnet temperatures led to fuel vaporization problems, particularly in warmer climates.

49. Flaps on the front wings open to allow access to the battery and screen washer bottle. They were discontinued for late 280Zs.

46

47

48

49

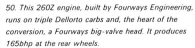

50. This 260Z engine, built by Fourways Engineering, runs on triple Dellorto carbs and, the heart of the conversion, a Fourways big-valve head. It produces 165bhp at the rear wheels.

51. A late works 240Z engine with crossflow head was originally fitted with fuel injection. Here it has been replaced by triple 44mm twin-choke Mikuni carbs. Note the oil cooler built into the right of the water radiator and battery on the right indicating a left-hand drive car.

52. This turbo system by Car Tech of Dallas offers around 320 bhp in 2.8-litre form. The fully intercooled turbo feeds through 3 twin-choke Mikuni carbs. Base turbo is by Rotomaster running at 12 psi.

53. Triple Mikuni carburettors on a works rally engine. Note the second set of bolt holes on the suspension turret – the sign of a genuine works shell. Either set of holes could be used, providing different camber settings for tarmac or forest suspension.

54

54. The Z432 scored its first victory at the Suzuka 1000km in May 1970. Seen here are four examples on the grid preparing for the start.

55. The Z432 (4 valves, 3 carburettors, 2 cams), which was used exclusively by the Japanese in the early racing days with reasonable success, is seen here at the Fuji 1000km on 26 July 1970.

56. Old Woking Service Station, which hosted the team in the UK, retained this ex-works car. Note the split front bumper, the centre section lowered to enable the auxiliary lamps to be recessed in the radiator opening.

55

56

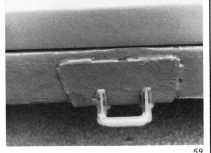

57

59

57. Rear of the Old Woking car. Note no reversing lights built into the rear cluster as on normal 240Zs.

58. High speed fuel filler on this late works rally car is accessed by lifting a flap on the tailgate. This flap is covered by the 'J' nationality plate.

59. This additional jacking point, welded onto the sill, was another feature of a works car.

60. The first rally victory in mainland Europe went to Antonio Carlos De Oliveira on the 1972 Rally of the Camellias in Portugal, where this photo was taken. This car was one of the original batch of works 240Zs built for the 1970 RAC Rally.

58

60

61

62

61. *This wonderfully atmospheric shot shows Rauno Aaltonen/Jean Todt sliding through the snow in the mountains above Monte Carlo in the 1972 rally where they finished third, the 240Z's best Monte result.*

62. *Photographed here on the 1973 T.A.P. Rally in Portugal is probably the most famous privately-entered 240Z, the Withers of Winsford car. This ex-works car, originally registered TKS 33 SA 696, was re-shelled after a roll on the '72 Scottish and survives today in a private collection.*

63. *This oddly-painted long-nosed 240ZG was snapped at the Japanese Fuji circuit 300km race on 18 March 1973. Note the ultra-thin fibreglass bonnet gaping at the sides due to higher pressure under the bonnet than above.*

63

64. Where else could this be but Le Mans? This ex-dealer team 260Z rally car was factory built on a 240Z shell (note rear lights). It was entered in the 1975 24-hours by works co-driver Hans Schuller but suffered serious differential problems.

65. 'Big Sam', Britain's most famous racing Z, had to fight hard for victory in the 1974 Modsports Championship. Based on Aaltonen's 1970 RAC Rally car, it is seen here having been rebuilt with an ex-Mehta Safari shell following a huge accident.

66. The 'Channel 9' team was a serious force in Australia, team driver Ross Dunkerton taking the Australian National Championship in 1975, '76 and '77, Alan Stean, the Queensland Z Club President, 'yumps' the ex-Dunkerton 240Z.

67a

67b

67a & b. Samuri entered both World Championship for Makes rounds in Britain in 1977. At Brands Hatch in September Win Percy had taken the Z up to seventh place when the race was stopped due to bad weather. These pictures show the Clive Richardson/Rod Grant car at Silverstone in May.

68. The Z Series domination of the SCCA C-Production Championship was total between 1970 and 1978, and was only broken by the model replacing the Z, the 280ZX. Here, Frank Leary is on his way to Championship victory in 1978 in his 280Z.

68

69a

69b

70

69 a & b. Don Kearney's SCCA C-Production racer, sponsored by, amongst others, the Marlow Datsun dealer, was known as the 'Crown Special'. Note the deep front spoiler with brake cooling ducts, and the roll cage braced forward onto the bulkhead (left). Also, the frameless doors and standard rear spoiler (right), which was the only rear spoiler permitted by the SCCA regulations.

70. 'Z Club' member Ian Pearce is seen here at Donington in 1983. His 1970 240Z, nicknamed Zorro, took a comfortable class win in the Post Historic Road Sports Championship which, effectively, is for unmodified cars. Note the non-European indicator/side lights of the earliest UK cars.